'John Schneider has written an outstanding book
and practice of psychoanalysis today. It is as if he
that allows the reader to cast his view on this f.
to an increasingly rich whole as the book procee
the pleasure of reading Schneider's work. I stror
interested in the mutative role of dreaming in the lives of every human being.'

—**Thomas Ogden** *is the author of 12 books of*
essays on the theory and practice of psychoanalysis, most
recently Coming to Life in the Consulting Room:
Toward a New Analytic Sensibility

'The inspiring strength of so many of Schneider's new ideas and views on dreams
and dreaming makes his book a new key step in the insurmountably complex, and
yet fascinating question of the meaning of thinking, understanding and knowing the
human mind. The language in which this book is written is the language of kindness,
ripened into a profound respect before the exceeding sensitivity of the human mind;
before the host of mysteries and enigmas weaving the human mind, even essentially
being the human mind. Such profound respect stands out as a crucial quality of the
analyst's reverie. As we move along his pages, we get the growing feeling of *hearing*
the music of his voice, of his thinking, of his deeply inspiring uncertainty, as well as
of the much he knows he does not know. This book lectures us all on how immensely
sensitive, exacting and often even frightening it is to sit behind a couch, for the much
we have to trust our fragile capacity for dreaming, and the little we can trust the
unfortunate much we believe we know.'

—**João Sousa Monteiro** *is a psychoanalyst in*
Lisbon, Portugal, and author of Bion's Theory of
Dreams: A Visionary Model of the Mind

Dreaming and Being Dreamt

In *Dreaming and Being Dreamt*, John Schneider illustrates the central concept of all emotional functioning: that we are most alive in our dreaming, and that it is dreaming that brings us to life.

Building upon the theoretical foundations of Ogden and Bion, the book explicates the way in which it is the unconscious goal of the patient, and the task of the analyst, to engage in dreaming the patient into existence in a fuller way than the patient has been able to dream. It goes on to develop the idea that all dreams are psychological works in progress, containing aspects of emotional experience that are entirely or partially too disturbing to dream on one's own. Each chapter of this book offers rich clinical exchanges between patient and analyst in analytic sessions. Schneider clearly shows how he dreams the analytic session with patients and the importance of "talking-as-dreaming" in contemporary psychoanalytic theory and practice.

With new insights on theory and rich clinical vignettes, this book will be indispensable for all psychoanalysts and psychoanalytic psychotherapists wanting to engage with the latest thinking on dreamwork.

John A. Schneider is a supervising and personal analyst at the Psychoanalytic Institute of Northern California. He is part of the Centre for the Advanced Study of the Psychoses. Previously, he served as the associate director of the Eating Disorders Program, Department of Psychiatry, Stanford University School of Medicine, and an assistant clinical professor in psychiatry. He was an associate clinical professor in psychiatry, University of California, San Francisco.

Dreaming and Being Dreamt

The Psychoanalytic Function of Dreams

John A. Schneider

Routledge
Taylor & Francis Group

LONDON AND NEW YORK

Designed cover image: 'La Perle' by Javier Vilató

First published 2023
by Routledge
4 Park Square, Milton Park, Abingdon, Oxon OX14 4RN

and by Routledge
605 Third Avenue, New York, NY 10158

Routledge is an imprint of the Taylor & Francis Group, an informa business

© 2023 John A. Schneider

British Library Cataloguing-in-Publication Data
A catalogue record for this book is available from the British Library

Every effort has been made to contact copyright-holders. Please advise the publisher of any errors or omissions, and these will be corrected in subsequent editions.

ISBN: 9781032471075 (hbk)
ISBN: 9781032471105 (pbk)
ISBN: 9781003384601 (ebk)

DOI: 10.4324/9781003384601

Typeset in Garamond
by Apex CoVantage, LLC

Also by John A. Schneider

Poetry

Swallowing the Light

For Donna,

and Lia and Peter

Contents

Acknowledgements   *x*

1 Introduction   1

2 From Freud's Dream-Work to Bion's Work of Dreaming: The
   Changing Conception of Dreaming in Psychoanalytic Theory   9

3 Bion's Thinking About Groups: A Study of Influence
   and Originality   29

4 Panic as a Form of Foreclosed Experience   48

5 Working With Pathological and Healthy Forms
   of Splitting   64

6 Experiences in K and –K   79

7 Janus-Faced Resilience in the Analysis of a Severely
   Traumatized Patient   93

8 Eating Disorders, Addictions, and Unconscious Fantasy   106

9 Signs and Symbols in *Dersu Uzala*   118

10 Dreaming the Truth of Experience: Heaven   124

Index   131

Acknowledgements

I would like to thank the *International Journal of Psychoanalysis* for permission to use the following papers in this volume:

> Experiences in K and –K. *International Journal of Psychoanalysis* 3(86): 8–25–839, 2005. Reprinted by permission of the publisher Taylor & Francis Ltd., www.tandfonline.com).
>
> From Freud's dream-work to Bion's work of dreaming: The changing conception of dreaming in psychoanalytic theory. *International Journal of Psychoanalysis* 3(91): 521–540, 2010. Reprinted by permission of the publisher Taylor & Francis Ltd., www.tandfonline.com).
>
> This paper was chosen as one of the ten most significant papers of the *International Journal of Psychoanalysis* in 2010 and reprinted in a French edition: 2011, *L'Anee Pschanalytique Internationalle*, 103–106.

I am grateful to the *Psychoanalytic Quarterly* for permission to use the following articles in this volume:

> Panic as a form of foreclosed experience. *Psychoanalytic Quarterly* 4(76): 1293–1316, 2007. Reprinted by permission of the publisher Taylor & Francis Ltd., www.tandfonline.com).
>
> Bion's thinking about groups: A study of influence and originality. *Psychoanalytic Quarterly* 2(84): 415–440, 2015. Reprinted by permission of the publisher Taylor & Francis Ltd., www.tandfonline.com).

The *Psychoanalytic Review* kindly granted permission to use the following articles in this volume:

> Janus-faced resilience in the analysis of a severely traumatized patient. *Psychoanalytic Review* 67: 869–867. © 2003 National Psychological Association for Psychoanalysis
>
> Dreaming the truth of experience: "Heaven." *Psychoanalytic Review* 5(92): pp. 777–785. © 2005 National Psychological Association for Psychoanalysis

Signs and symbols in *Dersu Uzula*. *Psychoanalytic Review* 1(96): pp. 173–180. © 2009 National Psychological Association for Psychoanalysis

I would like to thank the *Bulletin of the Menninger Clinic* for permission to use the following papers in this volume:

Eating disorders, addictions and unconscious fantasy. *Bulletin of the Menninger Clinic* 2(59): 177–179. © 1995 National Psychological Association for Psychoanalysis

Portions of this paper were presented at a symposium co-chaired by the author: "Psychoanalytic Work With Addictions: Views From Vienna and San Francisco," Vienna Psychoanalytic Institute, October 11, 1992.

Working with pathological and healthy forms of splitting: A case study. *Bulletin of the Menninger Clinic* 1(67): 32–49. © 2003 National Psychological Association for Psychoanalysis. An earlier version of this paper was read at The Second International Conference on Psychoanalytic Psychotherapy: Brescia, Italy, June 10, 1995. The paper was also published in International Psychoanalytic Research Project: Single Case Archive, 2013.

I would like to express gratitude to my friend Thomas Ogden, MD. I am deeply indebted to him for the generosity he has shown me and for his many insightful comments on this book.

I am also grateful to the members of the Wednesday Seminar.

I would like to express my appreciation to Ronda Davé Tycer, PhD for her diligent editing and proofreading throughout the preparation of this book.

Introduction

Dreaming and Being Dreamt: The Psychoanalytic Function of Dreams

The idea that we are most alive in our dreaming and that dreaming brings us to life lies at the heart of what I explore in this book. In each of the chapters I illustrate the way in which it is the unconscious goal of the patient, and the task of the analyst, to engage in dreaming the patient into existence in a fuller way than he has been able to (Ogden, 2004). The theoretical foundation on which I build my ideas is that developed by Wilfred Bion and Thomas Ogden. Bion re-conceptualized dreaming as an ongoing unconscious mental activity that continues while we are awake and asleep, and which is the central aspect of all emotional functioning. Ogden conceived of dreaming as synonymous with unconscious thinking that involves "the analyst making use of his own capacities for dreaming the emotional experience that is occurring in the session to facilitate the patient's efforts to dream his undreamable or incompletely dreamable dreams" (Ogden, 2017, p. 6–7).

Dreaming is a manifestation of the "psychoanalytic function" of the mind, according to Bion, a function that long preceded Freud, a function that will continue so long as human beings inhabit the world, regardless of whether there is a psychoanalyst around to discuss it. In my psychoanalytic practice the patient and I are always dreaming. I believe that all dreams are psychological works in progress and contain aspects of emotional experience that are entirely or partially too disturbing for patients to dream on their own. Patients bring their dreams to analysis with the hope of receiving help in completing the unconscious work by means of "talking as dreaming" (Ogden, 2007). In analytic sessions, I work to bring the dreaming in which the patient and I are engaged to a state in which it is integrated into the patient's personality in a way that helps him or her to live in a richer form than had been previously possible. In other words, I am not simply interested in expanding self-understanding. I am interested in facilitating the patient's recreating himself as a person who lives life differently from the way he had been previously able to live – that is, to live with a wider range of emotional experiences, richer relationships with others, a fertile imaginative life, and a life actively engaged with the larger world of which he is a part.

DOI:10.4324/9781003384601-1

While I greatly value Bion's and Ogden's ideas, this book is not an explication of their thoughts. Rather, it is a discussion with myself and the reader concerning how I think and re-think – learn and relearn – how to practice psychoanalysis.

Living One's Dreaming in Psychoanalysis

The line of thought I am developing in this book began with Bion (1962) and Ogden (1979), who transformed psychoanalysis into something quite different from what Freud (1900/1953) first introduced. Freud's primary goal in the practice of psychoanalysis was that of making conscious the derivatives of his patient's repressed unconscious. He relied heavily on dream interpretation to excavate patients' repressed impulses, fears, and desires. In Freud's dream interpretation, it is the analyst – not the patient – positioned between the patient's conscious and unconscious mind, who begins the work of interpreting the unconscious psychological conflicts represented in the patient's dreams.

In a radical departure from Freud, Bion suggested that therapists must take a more nuanced approach to understanding the patients' incomplete unconscious work. For Bion, dreaming is synonymous with unconscious thinking, and unconscious thinking is the richest form of thinking we are capable of. In describing the analyst's work, he imagined the therapist to be an archaeologist "when he thinks he has reached some potentially revealing object, and has to resort – not to a spade or a shovel – but [to] a camel-hair brush . . . something far gentler, far more revealing and less destructive . . ." (Bion, 1977, pp. 32–33), so as not to destroy what has been illuminated. To understand what his patients were unconsciously revealing in analysis, Bion relied on his reveries and his own emotional response to what his patients communicated. Reverie, for Bion, is the waking dreaming to which the analyst makes himself available as a way in which to intuit the unconscious aspect of what is occurring at any given moment in the analytic session. It is an indispensable part of analysis as a therapeutic process.

Freud had earlier acknowledged that there were other ways in which analysts become aware of their patients' unconscious experience. He identified extra-sensorial communication or telepathy as a viable pathway. "It is a very remarkable thing that the unconscious of one human being can act upon that of another, without passing through the conscious . . . the fact is incontestable" (1915/1957, p. 194). And in several publications (1921/1955a, 1922/1955b, 1933/1964) Freud elaborated this thinking. "There is . . . thought transference, which is close to telepathy . . . . It claims that mental processes in persons – can be transferred to another person through empty space without employing the familiar methods of communication by means of words and signs" (Freud, 1933/1964, p. 39). He suggested that patients and analysts might pick up unconscious thoughts through non-verbal bodily clues resulting from unconscious perception. Although Freud discussed unconscious communication from patient to analyst, he did not describe this sort of communication from analyst to patient. That aspect of psychoanalysis is an important part of the aspect of psychoanalysis with which I am engaged in this volume.

It was Klein's use of her concept of projective identification and her use of omnipotent phantasy (Klein, 1946/1952) that formed the theoretical framework with which she understood the projection by the patient of unconscious phantasy and primitive anxieties "*into*" (Klein, 1946/1952) the analyst. She believed that the patient expels, in unconscious phantasy, dangerous parts of the self "*into*" the analyst where he takes over the analyst from within. This phantasied unconscious evacuation of the dangerous part of the self is done not only in an effort to safeguard oneself against destructive internal objects, but also to enlist the other in helping to transform the projected part of the self into a form the patient might be able to think and make a safe part of oneself.

Building upon the ideas of Freud and Klein, Bion (1962, 1987, 1992) re-conceptualized the unconscious and conscious mind, making use of his own conception of dreaming, which to my mind, represents a paradigm shift in psychoanalytic thinking. From Bion's perspective, aspects of the mind communicate with one another in a mutually transformative way across a porous "contact barrier." He conceives of the contact barrier as functioning as a semi-permeable membrane that separates and regulates communication between the conscious and unconscious mind. This process of internal communication begins in the earliest stages of development and continues in the form of dreaming (both while we are asleep and awake) as a medium in which psychic change and growth occurs. As I have said, dreaming, for Bion, is synonymous with unconscious thinking, which is our richest form of thinking, far more generative than conscious secondary-process thinking or primary-process thinking in isolation from other types of thinking.

Over the past several decades, Ogden (1979, 2017) has elaborated Bion's theory of dreaming and extended Klein's theory of projective identification. Ogden added his own understanding that there is an "all important internal pressure" exerted on the analyst to comply emotionally with the patient's projections. He has in mind a pressure not simply to think as the patient wants him to think, but to experience himself as a figure in the patient's dream. In trying to conscript the analyst in this way, the patient exerts real interpersonal pressure on the analyst to comply with the projection. If the analyst is able to dream this experience instead of passively falling prey to the pressure, the analyst may be able to respond in a more mature way than the patient has been able to. The analyst, in this way, thinks the patient's unthinkable thoughts and through his interventions and his way of responding to the patient verbally and non-verbally, makes available to the patient a "thinkable" form of what had been unthinkable and un-integrate-able by the patient.

I will be developing ideas in this volume regarding the ways in which patients depend on the analyst's ability to receive and process projections by means of their ongoing reverie and self-analysis. When patient and analyst are able to engage in a process of dreaming together the experience of the analytic session, psychological growth may occur in both patient and analyst. By "dreaming together," I have in mind a process in which the analyst dreams the patient (for example, in reveries) in a slightly more mature state than what the patient is presently capable of achieving, and the patient dreams the analyst as a person or environment he most needed as a child.

To accomplish dreaming together, the analyst must be in moment-to-moment contact with "co-created dream thoughts" (Ogden, 2004) and must give himself over to his freely functioning imagination (reverie experience).

In the chapters that follow, I demonstrate what takes place in my work with patients as our minds engage in a process of dreaming up one another and dreaming together unconscious experience only the two of us can dream. We engage in a spoken and unspoken exchange in which aspects of the patient's life that have been shrouded in darkness – not even experienced by the patient – become lived in the analytic setting (to a large extent in the form of dreaming).

In some of the clinical experiences I will discuss, I made verbal interpretations concerning what I believed to be the leading edge of anxiety in the transference, only to realize I was in error and needed to change my way of talking to these patients. These lapses in my ability to participate in – or be alive to – the dreaming taking place between us represent instances in which I was consumed with anxiety that derived from my experience of being a figure in the patient's dreams. I was unable in these instances to dream the session *with* the patient and instead became psychically a figure in the patient's dream. To put this in other words, I had become an analyst being dreamed up by the patient in a form that was disturbing to me. Over time, in some of the analytic work I will present, I came to understand that I was experiencing myself as a figure in the patient's psychotic dream-thinking, a type of thinking that Bion (1962/1967) describes as the hallucinatory quality of a psychotic patient's dreaming. By hallucinatory quality, I mean those aspects of the patient's dream experiences that are so overwhelming they get evacuated into the analyst.

In other instances, I came to realize that instead of making use of genuine reverie, I was substituting rather mechanical thinking. I was in the grip of a defensive "knowing" when tolerance of uncertainty was what was called for. These experiences serve to demonstrate both the complexity and the importance of ongoing critical self-awareness concerning the nature of the thinking in which the analyst is engaged when – despite the fact he has the feeling he is dreaming – he is in fact engaged in a circular thought process that leads nowhere. An example of this occurred during my work with a patient going through a traumatic loss. My initial interventions involved a defensive, "overly" empathic, knowing, and understanding quality on my part. I had backed away from the intensity of feeling by engaging the patient in secondary process thinking rather than being present with the trauma, and dreaming with her, in a way that might allow her to begin living with her loss.

I would like now to give a sense of the chapter-by-chapter progression of this volume. I present in the second chapter two case discussions that illustrate how dreaming with the patient (dreaming up the patient and being dreamt up by the patient) allowed the patient to dream parts of previously undreamable emotional experience. In the first case, the patient was initially unable to "finish" his dreams, mostly post-traumatic nightmares, for fear that the disturbing parts he was unable to dream on his own (the hallucinatory parts) would lead to his losing his mind, and, consequently, losing himself, for what is a person without a mind. At one point in our work, he began to dream the disturbing parts of himself and was surprised when he woke up feeling more secure in himself than he felt previously. We were then able to talk about his earlier experiences of awaking in a state of fright when he had not been able to dream.

I then discuss the analysis of a patient in which it was necessary for me to dream in a way that was not visually representational as I was doing the unconscious psychological work necessary for the analysis to progress. The patient became emotionally withdrawn after her teenage son died in a car accident. She was unable to dream or make use of my interventions and felt the only resolution that would satisfy was the magical return of her son. Through my awareness of my somatic responses – cold numb fingertips and disturbed stomach – I eventually understood I was attempting to hold and digest for her what was unknowable and undigestable. Only then was I able to help her begin to dream what for both of us had been the most painful and undreamable: acknowledgement that her son was separate from her and dead.

Chapter 3 is an exploration of dream experience in a group. I take up one of Bion's (1959) most important, but least acknowledged, contributions to psychoanalytic theory – his study of the relationship between the mind of the individual (the ability to think) and the mentalities of the groups in which the individual is a member. For Bion, there was no distinction between the individual and the group. What happens to one member of the group happens to all of the members of the group; and what happens to the group happens to each individual member of the group. Regardless of our awareness or intent, we are always under the influence of the group. I have come to view an individual's group experiences as an important facet of the formation and maintenance of the patient's healthy and limiting psychic structure. I discuss ways in which group mentality is recognizable in the analysis of individuals and serves as a constant context for personal experience.

In the example I present, taken from the analytic literature, the patient was unable to dream the unconscious beliefs that were shaped by the groups, large and small, of which she was a member. The beliefs of the groups in which the patient lived influenced, for good and ill, the way she led her life. What's more, only when she became able to play with possibilities (which I consider a form of waking dreaming) concerning what she could do with these understandings could she make choices that felt like her own.

In Chapter 4, I present in detail a clinical experience in which a patient suffered from such intense anxiety as a manifestation of repressed conflict that he was unable to dream. The way he was best able to communicate with me was through the medium of bodily movement. For example, I once found him lying on the waiting room floor when I went to meet him. The patient struggled to transform undreamable experiences that had been relegated to his body. After a good deal of time, it was plain that the patient had not been able to grow in the analysis. I realized that my use of verbal interpretations as the principal mode of intervention was not effective. I began to make use of interventions informed by the reveries I experienced in response to his nonverbal (in large part bodily) communications. When I began to speak to him in response to (not about) my reverie experience, the patient grew better able to dream his experience with me. We became able to dream together experience previously somatized and isolated from dreaming on his own or with me. For example, I became more aware that the sound of what I was saying, as well as what I was conveying through the tone and speed of my voice, facial expressions, and other bodily movements, were as important as the meaning of my words. At other times, I would sit quietly with him when I had no words to express what I was feeling, as I did when I found him on the waiting room floor.

In Chapter 5, I illustrate through a detailed clinical account how I understand the concept of splitting, and how I make use of that concept in tracking changes in the patient and adjust my approach according to changes taking place in the patient. Initially, I failed to distinguish pathological splitting from healthy – but immature – forms of splitting. I considered splitting simply as a primitive defense and did not understand its role in early emotional development and healthy psychological maturation. In this chapter, I present both aspects of splitting – as a primitive defense (a facet of the paranoid-schizoid position) and as a healthy movement toward new and more complex object-relatedness.

My work with this patient evolved as we became better able to dream our own experiences and eventually to dream more mature unconscious experience together. I became better able to step out of the experience of the projective identification sufficiently to symbolize and talk to myself and eventually to the patient about what I had been dreaming/experiencing. This allowed me to not only speak about the experience I was dreaming up, but also to speak from it. When between sessions we experienced dreams that seemingly "corresponded with" the dream of the other, we became aware that we were unconsciously "on the same wavelength." In fact, we felt as if we were beginning to dream together what each of us was able to dream on his or her own. The patient was able to dream about being attracted to me, which she had been frightened about openly expressing, afraid I might reject her. And my dream experience contained similar feelings of affection and closeness toward the patient, which had not been previously acknowledged to myself, much less the patient. By expressing these thoughts, we were beginning to dream together what each of us had not been able to dream on our own.

In Chapter 6, I explore Bion's concept of K (knowing and needing to know) and –K (not knowing and needing not to know). I extend Bion's idea of –K as a distinctive experience driven by envy, to include forms of –K not driven by envy, and thus not necessarily pathological. At odds with the need to know (K) is the need, at times, to survive psychically by not knowing (–K).

I provide two examples of healthy use of –K. I first discuss the myth of Oedipus who wanted not to know (–K) the truth of his parentage (and the fact that he had unknowingly killed his father and married his mother). The ironic moral of the myth is that after "blinding" himself to these truths throughout his life, he came to know the truth (K) and literally blinded himself as a symbolic acceptance of the way he had had to survive the circumstances of his life. For Oedipus, not knowing was a healthy and humanly understandable use of (–K) as he attempted to live a life, a humanly tragic life.

The second example I offer of –K that is not pathological involves a severely disturbed patient who made use of not knowing (–K) in the service of psychic survival to the point of obliterating me through use of a negative hallucination (not believing she had ever met me when in fact we had begun working together in analysis). The patient could not distinguish between events occurring when awake from events occurring while waking dreaming, and confused the two during the analytic hours. In the analytic work with this patient, I created a way of talking that facilitated the patient's dreaming her experience during our sessions. For example, at one point, the patient described her relationship with her mother: "She says I have never been in her life." Feeling that the patient was unable to dream and to fully experience what she had just said, I told the patient, "I want to repeat something you just said: You . . . haven't . . . ever . . . been . . . in . . . her . . . life." Through my shift in tone of voice and change in cadence while repeating her words, and enunciating each syllable, I was emphasizing what she knew but could not yet fully know. I helped her bring to life parts of herself that seemed like a fiction to her. As she began taking the risk of entrusting me and herself with the primitive and psychotic aspects of herself – without "cracking up" – she was freer to experience what it was like to lose her mind with greater confidence that I could help her survive it without being killed or driven crazy myself.

In Chapter 7, I explore the double-edged quality of resilience and the possible drawbacks of developing resilience as a way of managing childhood trauma. I view resilience as the opposite of dreaming one's experience. I describe a patient's apparent childhood resourcefulness, fierce independence, and ability to take immediate adaptive action in response to terrible trauma. This reactivity on the patient's part foreclosed her dreaming and living the traumatic experience, which significantly limited her psychic development. Our work together involved coming to understand the nature of her resilience, which had kept her alive, but also stifled her healthy ability to dream her experience.

In Chapter 8, I describe how a bulimic patient exploited his body to express what he could not dream. The patient had to use his body to express what he could not experience psychologically because it was not represented symbolically. I illustrate in this clinical discussion the difference between being "lived by one's experience" and "living one's dreaming."

In the two chapters that follow, Chapters 9 and 10, I discuss two films in which I find compelling explorations of particular forms of human relatedness. I include these chapters because films make use of visual imagery to create meaning, as do dreams.

In Chapter 9, I examine the uncommon friendship and complex emotional bond between two figures in Akira Kurosawa's *Dersu Uzula*. In this film, a primitive trapper, Dersu Uzula, living in the rugged Siberian wilderness – the Ussurian taiga – observes from the safety of the forest the camp of Vladimir Arseniev, a Russian geographer and cartographer. Each of these men finds in the other aspects of self that he could not previously have dreamt of, much less fully experienced or expressed.

In Chapter 10, I discuss the film *Heaven* directed by Tom Tykwer, which artfully interlaces the dreamworld of the characters with their real world. Throughout the film, the viewer is taken back and forth between the characters' unconscious lives as they process elements of their real experience. The viewers, like the characters experience the fictional world as if in a dream, are never certain whether they are dreaming or perceiving reality.

References

Bion, W. R. (1959). *Experiences in groups*. Tavistock.

Bion, W. R. (1962). *Learning from experience*. Basic Books.

Bion, W. R. (1967). A theory of thinking. In *Second thoughts* (pp. 110–119). Aronson. (Original work published 1962)

Bion, W. R. (1977). *Taming wild thoughts*. Karnac Books.

Bion, W. R. (1987). *Clinical seminars and four papers*. Fleetwood Press.

Bion, W. R. (1992). *Cogitations* (F. Bion, Ed.). Karnac Books.

Freud, S. (1953). The interpretation of dreams. In J. Strachey (Ed. & Trans.), *The standard edition of the complete psychological works of Sigmund Freud* (Vol. 5, pp. 339–630). Hogarth Press. (Original work published 1900)

Freud, S. (1955a). Group psychology and the analysis of the ego. In J. Strachey (Ed. & Trans.), *The standard edition of the complete psychological works of Sigmund Freud* (Vol. 18, pp. 67–144). Hogarth Press. (Original work published 1921)

Freud, S. (1955b). Dreams and telepathy. In J. Strachey (Ed. & Trans.), *The standard edition of the complete psychological works of Sigmund Freud* (Vol. 18, pp. 195–220). Hogarth Press. (Original work published 1922)

Freud, S. (1957). The unconscious. In J. Strachey (Ed. & Trans.), *The standard edition of the complete psychological works of Sigmund Freud* (Vol. 14, pp. 159–215). Hogarth Press. (Original work published 1915)

Freud, S. (1964). Dreams and occultism. In J. Strachey (Ed. & Trans.), *The standard edition of the complete psychological works of Sigmund Freud* (Vol. 22, pp. 31–57). Hogarth Press. (Original work published 1933)

Klein, M. (1952). Notes on some schizoid mechanisms. In M. Klein, S. Isaacs, P. Heimann, & J. Riviere (Eds.), *Developments of psychoanalysis*. Hogarth Press. (Original work published 1946)

Ogden, T. H. (1979). On projective identification. *International Journal of Psychoanalysis*, *60*, 357–373.

Ogden, T. H. (2004). This art of psychoanalysis: Dreaming undreamt dreams and interrupted cries. *International Journal of Psychoanalysis*, *85*, 857–877.

Ogden, T. H. (2007). Elements of analytic style: Bion's clinical seminars. *International Journal of Psychoanalysis*, *88*, 1185–1200.

Ogden, T. H. (2017). Dreaming the analytic session: A clinical essay. *Psychoanalytic Quarterly*, *86*, 1–20.

2

From Freud's Dream-Work to Bion's Work of Dreaming

The Changing Conception of Dreaming in Psychoanalytic Theory

"Wir haben die Kunst, damit wir nicht ander Wahrheit zugrunde geben."
["We have art so that we shall not be destroyed by the truth."]

– Nietzsche (n.d.)

I

Dreams paradoxically protect us from and inform us about unknown truths. Dreams paint a timeless montage, brushed freely by remnants of past, present, and possible future experience. The true meaning of a dream can never be known and never told. Dreams are works in progress that – if we are open to them – give us a chance to come to grips with truths that we feel least capable of facing. But those truths are always more than we can bear: in every dream, to some degree, we evade much of what is true to our emotional experience.

For some time now, it has seemed to me that psychoanalysis has moved its focus away from dreams. I think that this, at least in part, reflects reluctance by practicing psychoanalysts to think about dreams in ways that go beyond Freud's momentous contribution. Simply put, Freud's towering legacy dissuaded subsequent theorists from re-considering dream-work from new perspectives that require of the contemporary analyst nothing less than a paradigm shift.

Bion makes this shift by putting dreaming at the core of psychological functioning, and moving the emphasis in dream theory "from the symbolic meaning of dreams to the *process of dreaming*" (Ogden, 2007). He is concerned more with the *way* we dream than with the dream's symbolic *content* (Bion, 1962). Dreaming, for Bion, involves the pursuit of truth through thinking and feeling. He believes that the driving force of human development is the search for truth and that the mind is developed through dreaming as we strive to discover what is real about our experience.

In this chapter, I will develop two of Bion's ideas concerning dreaming: (1) the idea that aspects of all dreams are works in progress that allow some access to veiled truths about ourselves (Bion, 1962); and (2) the idea that all dreams also contain elements that are not works in progress and are the equivalent of visual hallucinations, an idea that Bion proposed to himself (in his *Cogitations*, 1992) but never developed or published during his lifetime.

DOI:10.4324/9781003384601-2

II

Freud's Dream-Work and Bion's Work of Dreaming

Freud rescued the study of dreams from mythmakers, seers, neurologists, and purveyors of the daemonic.[1] He brought to the understanding of dreams a scientific approach offering new possibilities for exploring and organizing previously unknown and unknowable depths of the unconscious.

Freud considered *The Interpretation of Dreams* (1900/1953a) to be "the most valuable of all the discoveries it has been my good fortune to make. Insight such as this falls to one's lot but once in a lifetime" (p. xxxii). But when Freud introduced his structural model in *The Ego and the Id* (1923/1961b), many felt that it was "so unrelated to dream analysis as to have appreciably diminished the importance of clinical emphasis on the dream" (Waldhorn, 1967, p. 52). The Kris Study Group suggested that Freud led psychoanalysts away from a focus on dreams by shifting emphasis from the topographic model to the structural model (Waldhorn, 1967).[2]

Curiously, Freud's contributions were so revolutionary that they had the effect of halting further theorizing about dreaming. Freud regretted that his analytic colleagues did not share his enthusiasm for dreams. Many contemporary analysts would disagree with Freud's view that dreams hold a "special place" (Freud, 1933/1964b, p. 7) in the practice of psychoanalysis, offering access to "material otherwise unavailable" (p. 7), and believe that the dream is "simply one of many types of material useful for analytic inquiry" (Waldhorn, 1967, p. 57). Freud (1933/1964a) stated in his *New Introductory Lectures:* "The analysts behave as though they had no more to say about dreams, as though there was nothing more to be added to dream theory" (p. 8) (i.e., as if Freud had already said it all). Freud's disappointment is evident in this statement, but there is also a strong invitation for psychoanalysts to carry forward his investigation of dreams.

Bion's re-conceptualization of the theory of dreaming is perhaps one of the great paradigm shifts in psychoanalytic history. Bion viewed his work on dreaming as "a legitimate extension of an opening for investigation which Freud made but did not follow up" (Bion, 1992, p. 73). While Freud's dream theory provides a model for conceiving of the way in which derivatives of the unconscious become conscious, Bion's dream theory provides a model for how the mind processes emotional experience, giving it meaning. He construes dreaming as the unconscious processing of emotional experience, which occurs continuously and simultaneously with conscious thinking.

In considering differences between Freud's and Bion's theories of dreaming, confusion often arises because they use similar terms to refer to different phenomena. Bion expanded upon Freud's theory of dream-work "without being restricted . . . by an existing penumbra of ideas" (Bion, 1962, p. 2), but at the same time without entirely setting aside Freud's ideas in favor of his own. He wrote, "The term 'dream' I shall always use for the phenomenon described by Freud under that term" (Bion, 1992, p. 95). And again, "The title 'dreamwork' has already a meaning of great value. I wish to extend some of the ideas already associated with it and to limit others" (Bion, 1992, p. 62). These sentences taken from Bion's personal notebook, *Cogitations* (Bion, 1992) (which he never intended to be published), demonstrate how Bion was able to extend the intended meaning of what we think of as a "dream" by considering the phenomenon from new perspectives.

In the following historical, theoretical, and clinical overview, I will focus on Freud's idea that the analyst – not the patient – begins the work of interpreting the unconscious psychological conflict in dreams, and will demonstrate this by examining his work with the "Dental Stimulus Dream" (Freud, 1900/1953a). I will then discuss Bion's concept of dreaming as our most fundamental way of processing emotional experience. In this connection, I will present a close reading of a paragraph taken from *Cogitations* (Bion, 1992) in which Bion steps back to question his own theory of dreaming, and, in so doing, leaves open for consideration the possibility that dreaming (from a vantage point different from all of Bion's other vantage points) is a reflection of emotional work that has come to a halt. Finally, by combining several of Bion's ways of viewing dreaming, I will propose that all dreams can be viewed as unconscious thinking-in-progress but contain elements that the dreamer is completely unable to dream.

III

Freud's Dream-Work

Most readers today are surprised to realize that, for Freud (1900/1953b), dreams serve one purpose and one purpose only: they are the "guardians of sleep" (p. 678) – a purely physiological process. Freud (1916/1961a) states: "[A] dreamless sleep is the best, the only proper one. There ought to be no mental activity in sleep" (p. 89). He reiterated this belief almost a decade later when he wrote, "There is only one useful task, only one function, that can be ascribed to a dream, and that is the guarding of sleep from interruption" (Freud, 1923/1961b, p. 127).

Freud is saying that the anxiety associated with the threat of the "return of the repressed" is so great that a person awakes from his dreams. The metaphor is a pressure-valve metaphor rather than a metaphor of unconscious transformation that mediates psychological growth (in contrast to Bion's digestive-system metaphor that I will discuss later).

> The state of sleep does not wish to know anything of the external world; it takes no interest in reality, or only so far as abandoning the state of sleep – waking up – is concerned . . . all the essential characteristics of dreams are determined by the conditioning factor of sleep.
>
> (Freud, 1915/1957, p. 234)

Dreams, as "guardians of sleep," serve the psychological function of keeping sleep from being overwhelmed by disturbing thoughts. If repressed infantile wishes exert pressure for access to thinking and are uncensored or poorly disguised, they enter the preconscious in a form that is so disturbing as to wake the person up.

Freud does not believe that by dreaming the dreamer does psychological work that helps deal with unsettling emotional experience; rather, he believes that dreaming dissipates the threat of overwhelming anxiety caused by the tension of repressed sexual impulses originating in childhood. This view suggests that human emotional development is driven by instincts (experienced as sexual impulses and their derivatives) and that the taming of sexual tension and expression is the primary developmental force.

Freud believed that we dream only in sleep when the freedom of visual representation that comes with diminished censorship and a state of disconnection of the mind from voluntary musculature allow derivatives of the repressed to appear in dreams. The dream safeguards sleep by acting as a safety valve, allowing sleep to continue by letting off just enough tension from unconscious drives. If too much libidinal or aggressive energy is released, the capacity for symbol formation through dreaming is exceeded. When unconscious tension builds to such intensity, it wakes the person up. Pressure is transferred from one part of the mind to the other, but the underlying emotional tension continues to exist unless and until *the analyst* makes an interpretation that helps to resolve the unconscious conflict to which it has given rise. The work being done during dreaming alone is limited to monitoring and regulating the "return of the repressed."[3]

Freud also explored the way the preconscious and unconscious minds communicate with each other during dreaming. He made clear divisions between primary and secondary process thinking, unconscious and conscious states, and the states of being asleep and being awake (see Freud, 1911/1958). During sleep, there is a disconnection from the logic (and musculature) of waking life; the focus of one's attention is turned entirely to managing one's internal life (Freud, 1903/1953b, p. 608).

Dream-work translates the unconscious (latent) content such as childhood sexual wishes, fears, and conflicts into the manifest content according to principles of *condensation*: "the first achievement of the dream-work" (Freud, 1916/1961a, p. 171), which collapses several concepts into one for purposes of disguise; *displacement*: "replacing something by an allusion . . . [which is] more remote"(Freud, 1916/1961a, p. 174); and *representation*: "transforming thoughts into visual images"(Freud, 1916/1961a, p. 175). Through these disguising mental operations, forbidden wishes are altered in such a way as to give their unconscious derivatives "free access to the conscious [mind]" (Freud, 1915/1957, p. 149). Dream-work accomplishes censorship, editing, and compromising, which allows the person to dissipate the sleep-disturbing tension associated with infantile wishes by "smuggling" them (past the censor) into the preconscious and conscious mind. There is no psychological work (yielding maturational advance) inherent in the disguising and smuggling function of dream-work.

In Freud's dream interpretation, the analyst – positioned between the conscious and the unconscious – interprets the patient's dream, by reversing the direction of dream-work, beginning with the manifest content and working backward to the latent material (Freud, 1916/1961a). Dream-work is "the work which transforms the latent dream into the manifest one; the work which proceeds in the contrary direction, which endeavors to arrive at the latent dream from the manifest, is our [the analyst's not the patient's] work of interpretation . . . [which] seeks to undo the dream-work" (Freud, 1916/1961a, p. 170).

The dream-thoughts and dream-content are presented to us like two versions of the same subject matter in two different languages. Or, more properly the dream-content seems like a transcript of the dream-thoughts into another mode of expression, whose characters and syntactic laws it is our [the analyst's] business to discern by comparing the original and the translation. Thoughts are immediately comprehensible as soon as we [the analyst] have learnt them.

(Freud, 1900/1953a, p. 277)

With this statement Freud is clearly emphasizing the analyst's primary role in interpreting the patient's dreams and de-emphasizing the role of the patient in interpreting or understanding his dreams on his own, which is at odds with the way most analysts currently think about dreaming.

The analyst can, by linking the manifest content to latent content, do something more with the dream than the patient is able to do on his own. The analyst's skill in translating the dream's latent content is described by Freud: "When the patient runs out of associations . . . we intervene on our own; we fill in the hints, draw undeniable conclusions, and give explicit utterances to what the patient has only touched on in his associations" (Freud, 1933/1964b, p. 12). Once achieved, "interest in the dream . . . is for the most part at an end" (Freud, 1933/1964b, p. 17); "[like] the solution to a jigsaw puzzle, there is no alternative solution" (Freud, 1933/1964b, p. 12). This and the following comments reflect the degree to which Freud sees the work of dream interpretation as almost exclusively the domain of the analyst. The analyst "call[s] up ideas that occur to the dreamer till you have penetrated from the substitute to the genuine thing and, on the ground of your own [the analyst's] knowledge, replacing the symbols by what they mean" (Freud, 1916/1961a, p. 170).

Not only did Freud say that the patient does no logical productive thinking in the act of dreaming, he also believes that even the patient's associations to the dream do not involve secondary process thinking:

Everything that appears in dreams as the ostensible activity of the formation of judgment is to be regarded not as intellectual achievement of the dream-work but as belonging to the material of the dream-thought and as having been lifted from them into the manifest content of the dream. . . . I can even carry this assertion further. Even judgments made after waking up on a dream that has been remembered, and the feelings called up in us by the reproduction of such a dream, form part . . . of the latent content of the dream and are to be included in the [analyst's] interpretation.

(Freud, 1900/1953b, p. 445)

Here, Freud seems to further separate primary- from secondary-process thinking by viewing even the associations that the patient gives after waking as part of the latent content of the dream.

One of Freud's most quoted ideas – "*The interpretation of dreams is the royal road to a knowledge of the unconscious activities of the mind*" (Freud, 1900/1953b, p. 608) – often is misleadingly shortened to: "Dreams are the royal road to the unconscious." This shorthand obscures the critical idea that Freud was emphasizing, namely, that *the analyst's interpretation of dreams* (not dreams themselves or the patient's interpretation of his own dream) offers the possibility for understanding unconscious mental activity of the dreamer. The patient's primary roles in dream analysis are that of free-associating, and later thinking and speaking in secondary process logic, in response to the analyst's interpretation of the dream.

IV

Freud's Work With a Dream

In *The Interpretation of Dreams*, Freud (1900/1953b) presents the "Dental Stimulus Dream," which illustrates the importance that Freud attributed to the analyst's interpretation of dreams and how all interpretations unveil repressed sexual memories, thoughts, desires, and fears. A dream dreamt by a patient of Otto Rank's colleague provides Freud with an opportunity to demonstrate how his theory of dreaming works.

Freud's dream interpretation (carried out through Rank's colleague) follows the steps of dream formation in reverse, working backward from the manifest content – a visit to the dentist to have a tooth pulled. In his preamble, Freud (1900/1953b) tells the reader that the dream is a typical dream in which a "dental stimulus" (p. 387) is used to represent repressed infantile sexuality.

Having thus guided the reader in how to think about the dream, Freud presents the dream sent to him by Rank from his colleague's patient:

> A short time ago I had a dream that I was at the dentist and he was drilling a back tooth in my lower jaw. He worked on it so long that the tooth became useless. He then seized it with a forceps and pulled it out with an effortless ease that excited my astonishment. He told me not to bother about it, for it was not the tooth that he was really treating, and put it on the table, where the tooth (as it now seemed to me, an upper incisor) fell apart into several layers. I got up from the dentist's chair, went closer to it with a feeling of curiosity, and raised a medical question, which interested me. The dentist explained to me, while he separated out the various portions of the strikingly white tooth and crushed them up (pulverized them) with an instrument, that it was connected with puberty and that it was only before puberty that teeth came out so easily.
>
> (Freud, 1900/1953b, p. 388)

After reporting the dream, Rank states, "Experiences and thoughts from the previous day provide material for an interpretation of the dream" (Freud, 1900/1953b, p. 389). The patient revealed that recently he had had dental treatment and was having continual pain in a tooth in the lower jaw – where, in reality, a dentist had worked longer than the patient had liked. On the day of the dream, he had been to the dentist, who suggested that the pain was probably caused by a tooth that needed to be pulled – a "wisdom tooth."

Rank was pleased with his colleague's interpretation and reported to Freud that: "So much for the interpretation [of masturbatory desires] put forward by my colleague, which is most enlightening, and to which, I think, no objections can be raised. I have nothing to add to it" (Freud, 1900/1953b, p. 391). Having "extracted" the repressed material and having offered it to the patient in the form of an interpretation, the analyst's work with the dream is complete, and we are told that Freud, Rank, Rank's colleague, and the patient are in agreement.

Freud leaves the reader with his thesis: dreams are a product of disguised, unconscious infantile sexual wishes that require the analyst to translate the manifest content of the dream into the "language" of the latent content. I would add to Freud's formulations the idea that the latent content is originally presented to the preconscious and conscious mind in the "language" of dream imagery and narrative. So when the analyst translates the manifest content of a dream "back" into the language of the latent content, he is in fact translating the language of latent content into a verbally symbolic form for the first time.

This verbally symbolized version of the latent content is then presented as an interpretation to the patient and "makes the motive force . . . nothing other than the masturbatory desires of the pubertal period" (Freud, 1900/1953b, p. 385).

By laying out his step-by-step-method, Freud left future generations of psychoanalysts a powerful model for the interpretation of dreams.

V

Bion's Re-Conception of Dreaming

[S]omebody here should, instead of writing a book called *The Interpretation of Dreams*, write a book called *The Interpretation of Facts*, translating them into dream language – not just as a perverse exercise [by the analyst], but in order to get a two-way traffic [on the "royal road"].
(Bion, 1980b, p. 31)

In this statement, Bion adds to Freud's conception of working with dreams (the "interpretation of dreams") his own way of working with emotional experience (the "interpretation of facts") – which allows for "two-way traffic" between conscious and unconscious thinking. For Bion, psychoanalysis is, most fundamentally, the work of interpreting facts, raw sensory impressions – the elementary "facts"; not the work of interpreting dreams, because dreams are themselves the way we have already interpreted the facts – the way we have successfully thought about our emotional experience. Dreams are the interpretation of the facts of the dreamer's current emotional reality, the "experience of external or internal psychic reality" (Bion, 1992, p. 45).

The underlying premise of Bion's conceptualization of dreaming is that dreaming is the primary psychoanalytic function of the mind (Ogden, 2004), and consequently, when we are unable to dream, we are unable to do essential conscious and unconscious psychological work with our emotional experiences. "Failure to eat, drink, or breathe properly has disastrous consequences for life itself" (Bion, 1962, p. 42). "Failure to use the emotional experience produces a comparable disaster in the development of the personality; . . . [which includes] psychotic deterioration . . . as [the] death of the personality" (Bion, 1962, p. 42). He wrote:

> The "felt need" [the patient's need to render meaningful his emotional experience] is very important; if it is not given due significance and weight, the true disease [psychopathology = inability to dream] of the patient is being neglected, is obscured by the analyst's insistence on interpretation of the dream [i.e., the analyst, in doing the work of dream interpretation, loses sight of the fact that the patient cannot dream].
>
> (Bion, 1992, p. 184)

For a period of time, Bion used his metaphorical concept of alpha function as a way to conceptualize dreaming. He describes "alpha function" as an "unknown" (Bion, 1962, p. 38) yet-to-be-discovered set of mental functions, which "transforms the sense impressions [beta elements] related to an emotional experience into alpha elements" (1962, p. 17). Only after alpha function has turned beta elements into alpha elements do they congeal into a dream-thought suitable for dreaming. "Alpha function transforms sense impressions into alpha elements, which . . . may . . . be identical with the visual images . . . in dreams . . ." (Bion, 1962, p. 7), and provide the mind material with which to create dream-thoughts (Bion, 1962/1967, p. 115), and give emotional problems a symbolic form in which the person may think/dream them (Bion, 1962; Meltzer, 1983; Grotstein, 2000, 2002, 2007; Ogden, 2007).

Bion used the term "dream-thoughts" to refer to the product of the accretion of alpha elements (Bion, 1962). The dream-thought is composed of linked elements of experience derived from and representing different facets of an emotional problem that needs to be resolved. When the emotional experience remains in the form of unlinked beta elements, they constitute "undigested facts" that cannot be used in the formation of dream-thoughts (Bion, 1962, p. 6).

Beta elements "are not amenable for use in constructing dream-thoughts, and consequently, are amenable only for evacuation in projective identification" (Bion, 1962, p. 6), psychosomatic illness, severe perversions, and so on. Projective identification involves psychic evacuation as well as communication: "The patient, even at the outset of life, has contact with reality sufficient to enable him to act in a way that engenders in the mother feelings that he does not want, or which he wants the mother to have"(Bion, 1962, p. 31).

Bion concludes that the psychotic's thought disorder and confusion are related to an inability to dream, and said [in an interpretation he made to a psychotic patient], "Without phantasy or dreams you have not the means with which to think out your problems" (Bion, 1962, pp. 25–26). Because psychotic patients are unable to discriminate between conscious and unconscious experience or to differentiate an actual event in reality from a hallucination or a dream or a fantasy, their dreams are not forms of genuine thinking and do not contribute to psychological growth.

In other words, the "dreams" of the psychotic are "dreams that are not dreams": no genuine unconscious psychological work is done, and the patients cannot learn from the experience being hallucinated in sleep. In "On Hallucination" (1967, p. 78), Bion suggests that the "[psychotic's] dreams showed so many characteristics of the hallucination that . . . experiences of hallucination in the consulting room might serve to throw light on the psychotic dream" (1967, p. 78).

Bion (1962/1967) believes that both psychotic and non-psychotic aspects of the personality contribute to all dreams. He identified parts of personalities that seem to be incapable of true dreaming, not only in psychotic and borderline psychotic personalities but also in psychotic parts of the [normal] personality (Bion, 1962, p. 54). These are the parts of the self (even in the healthiest of people) that are dominated by beta/hallucinatory elements, and which are thus unable to think, learn from experience, or do psychological work.

Analysts who give patients interpretations of their dreams may be missing the fact that some of the dreams or parts of the dreams are disturbing psychic events occurring during sleep that appear to be dreams but are not dreams and do not "warrant the name dream" (Bion, 1962; Ogden, 2005). In these dream-like imagistic experiences, neither the patient nor the analyst has genuine associations, and the experience achieves little or no unconscious psychological work.

For Bion, the development of the ability for unconscious psychological work begins in the mother-infant relationship, when the mother's mind is able to help transform the infant's beta elements into a form that the infant's rudimentary alpha function is able to process.

"Undreamable dreams" or undreamable parts of dreams might be thought of as beta elements not yet transformed by alpha function – perhaps a residue of what was undreamable in the mother-infant situation or in later disturbing or traumatic emotional experiences.

Undreamt dream-thoughts remain as split-off pockets of psychosis (Bion, 1962). Ogden (2007) refers to this as "undreamable experience" resulting from any of a number of external traumas or intra-psychic forces that "remain with the individual as undreamt dreams in such forms as psychosomatic illness, split-off psychoses, 'dis-affected' states (McDougall, 1984), 'pockets of autism' (Tustin, 1982), 'severe perversions' (de M'Uzan, 1984), and addictions" (Ogden, 2007, p. 577). In these non-dreams, no psychological work is being done; instead, symptoms are generated that are derived from the foreclosed, non-symbolic experience (de M'Uzan, 1984; Schneider, 2003a, 2003b).

Bion (1962) considered these non-dreams to be a form of non-thinking involving

the use of the visual images of the dream for purposes of control and ejection of unwanted . . . emotional experience. The visual image of the dream is then felt as a hallucinated – that is to say, artificially produced – container intended to hold in, imprison, inoculate the emotional experience the personality feels too feeble to contain without danger of rupture, and so to serve as a vehicle for the evacuatory process.
(Bion, 1992, p. 67)

Ogden describes this as the contained (the dream thought) overwhelming and destroying the container (the capacity for dreaming) (Ogden, 2004, p. 4) Dreaming is a containing (i.e., thinking) function; but if dream-thoughts are sufficiently disturbing, they (the contained) can overwhelm the capacity for dreaming (i.e., the container).

Implicit in Bion's work is the idea that beta elements that are not narrativized are split off and evacuated or remain unthought emotional experiences. The emotional problem to be solved remains a stagnant, but troubling, psychological presence – because evacuation is never complete. There is, for an instant before evacuation, recognition of the undreamable experience, which leaves a disturbing impression (in the psychotic part of the personality) that presses for continuing the work (in analysis). Even in "healthy dreams," there are both psychotic and non-psychotic elements: "contact with reality is never entirely lost [evacuated] . . . the withdrawal from reality is an illusion, not a fact, and arises from the deployment of projective identification" (Bion, 1962, p. 46).

In a significant break from Freud, Bion contends that there is no difference between unconscious processing of experience while we are awake and unconscious processing of experience while we are asleep; we are always dreaming our emotional experience. Bion writes: "Freud (1933/1964b, pp. 26–27) says Aristotle states that a dream is the way the mind works in sleep: I say it is [also] the way it works when awake" (Bion, 1992, p. 43).

> An emotional experience occurring in sleep . . . does not differ from the emotional experience occurring during waking life in that the perceptions of the emotional experience have in both instances to be worked upon by [unconscious] alpha function before they can be used for dream thoughts.
>
> (Bion, 1962, p. 6)

That is, both waking and sleeping experiences are subjected to the same unconscious thinking process by which psychological work is done. The non-psychotic part of the personality is always making meaning of internal and external experience as it (1) transforms beta into alpha elements, (2) links alpha elements in the formation of dream-thoughts, and (3) thinks one's dream-thoughts in the form of dreaming.

Bion believes that dreaming is thinking about emotional experience and that, in the process of dreaming, conscious lived experience is made available to the unconscious for psychological work. Freud, on the other hand, believes that the unconscious mind is not capable of real thinking (logical, secondary process thinking), and that the function of "dream-work" (Freud, 1900/1953a) is to safeguard sleep by protecting the conscious mind against the "return of the repressed." Bion believes that patients who bring a dream to an analytic session have already begun doing psychological work in the very act of dreaming. Patients bring their dreams to analysts not to have their dreams interpreted but to continue dreaming with the analyst aspects of the dreams that they have not been able fully to dream on their own.

Bion felt that Freud's theory of "consciousness" was incomplete and suggested that "the conscious and unconscious [which are] constantly produced together do function as if they were binocular [and] therefore capable of correlation and self-regard" [i.e., self-awareness] (Bion, 1962, p. 54). In other words, they constitute different vertices from which each can look at, and benefit from, the other. In health, we are able to move freely between the conscious and unconscious mind having a two-way conversation through the semi-permeable "contact barrier" (1962, p. 17) of dreaming, and able to be conscious of some elements of experience, and unconscious of others, while allowing communication between the two.

Echoing Freud, Bion states that while we are asleep, we shut off most sense impressions coming from the external world and turn our full attention inward and that this makes sleep an ideal time for unconscious thinking of one's emotional experience (dreaming):

> One of the reasons why sleep is essential is to make possible, by suspension of consciousness, the emotional experiences that the personality would not permit itself to have during conscious waking life . . . for conversion into alpha-elements and a narrative form (Bion, 1992, p. 150).
>
> I wonder if dreams, that is, the actual emotional experiences are not the emotional experiences I do not have, or cannot allow myself to have, during wakefulness.
>
> (Bion, 1992, p. 149)

VI

Bion's Undeveloped Idea of Dreams as Works in Progress

> I think it is important to find ["the answers"] out for your selves. I try to give you a chance to fill the gap left by me.
>
> (Bion, 1980a, p. 5)

Bion believes that in order to advance psychoanalytic theory, one must have the freedom to think based upon one's unique experience. In accord with this belief, in his writing, Bion intentionally presents ideas without offering the certainty of conclusions, and leaves us with a theory of dreaming that includes an invitation for readers to do something of their own with his ideas (Schneider, 2005a, 2005b, 2005c). "The reader may find the effort to clarify these [obscure ideas] for himself is rewarding and not simply work that has been forced on him because I have not done it myself" (Bion, 1962, p. ii).

Much of my thinking about dreams as "works in progress" is derived from thoughts that Bion considered but never developed. In virtually the entirety of Bion's published writings, he thought of dreaming as the process by which emotional experience is given meaning. That is to say, dreaming is the process by which problematic raw emotional experience (registered as beta elements) is changed into meaningful emotional experience (alpha elements) with which the dreamer can then do unconscious psychological work. The dream is the representation of an emotional experience in the process of resolution.

However, in the last paragraph of his August 10, 1959, entry in *Cogitations*, Bion speculates that this conception of dreaming may be *entirely wrong*. Perhaps our dreams are comprised exclusively of emotional experiences that we have been unable to think about unconsciously, and which we are therefore evacuating through projective iden-tification in the form of dreams.

> I suggest what is ordinarily reported as a dream [even in health] should be regarded by us as a sign of indigestion, but not simply physical indigestion. Rather, it should be taken as a symptom of mental indigestion. Or, to phrase it more exactly, as a sign when a patient reports a dream to us and we are satisfied that he means by this what we all ordinarily understand by a dream – that there has been a *failure* of dream-work alpha.[4] The failure of course may be due to precisely such causes as the use of visual imagery in the service of projective identification which I have just been describing [in psychotic patients], but there are other more common causes of failure of dream-work alpha, and there are also degrees of frequency with which the patient resorts to the use of dream imagery in the service of projective identifica-tion. *Investigation of the dream [all dreams] as a symptom of a failure of dream-work alpha means that we have to reconsider the series of hypotheses that I have grouped together under the heading of dream-work alpha.*
>
> (Bion, 1992, p. 68) [italics added])

Here, using one of his favorite metaphors for thinking – the digestive system – Bion says that the dream may be a "symptom of mental indigestion" that reveals the fact that some emotional experience has not yet been fully digested. Bion states that when a patient reports a dream, "it should be taken as a symptom" of "a failure of dream-work alpha." Adding to his theory that dreaming is unconscious emotional thinking, he suggests that all dreams may, at least in part, reflect an inability to pro-cess the emotional experience. Rather than representing healthy emotional process-ing, the dream brought to the analyst, even by a relatively healthy patient, may in part represent the breakdown of emotional processing resulting in the use of "visual imagery in the service of projective identification," i.e., a form of visual hallucina-tion. Dreams may reveal stalls and limitations in the unconscious thinking process.

Bion implies that there is no reason to have (make) a dream of the sort that the dreamer may remember on waking if the dreamer has already accomplished in uncon-scious thinking (while asleep) what he needed to accomplish. From this perspective, it is the unsuccessful dream, the unthought, undreamt dream-thought that is evacuated into visual dream imagery and then brought to the analyst (in its dead-end state) for help in thinking what has been, to that point, a nonexistent, or perhaps barely begun, thinking process.

Contrary to the idea he had been working on (and a good deal of what he had pre-viously believed about dreaming), Bion considers here the possibility that all dreams (even the dreams of healthy people) may not reflect unconscious thinking about emotional experience but may instead represent the failure of unconscious thinking which manifests itself in the form of (visual) hallucinatory or evacuatory processes.

Bion is able to say two contradictory things because he is looking at dreaming from different vertices, where the assumptions of one perspective are not the same as the assumptions of the other. Bion demonstrates the essential process underlying his work from beginning to end – that he (and the rest of us) must be free to think every thought from different vertices, no matter how objectionable, illogical, or contradictory they may seem. As if talking to himself, Bion poses the question: What kind of thinking would dreaming be? (Bion, 1992, p. 67). He tries out the idea that dreaming is generative thinking – "For the true dream *is* felt as life promoting" (p. 67). But then he seems to be asking himself, What if I think of dreaming as a manifestation of all that cannot be dreamt or thought unconsciously? (p. 67). That would change everything. Bion is trying out the idea that dreams are visual hallucinations. "It [the visual hallucinatory experience in sleep] is suspect as being only the *appearance* of a life-promoting phenomenon and so the patient's sense of being unable to dream is unaffected" (p. 66–67), i.e., the patient is correct in his sense of being unable to dream. Bion is suggesting that patients naturally guard against hallucinatory parts of dreams, which require "the mind of another" to be dreamt. Finally, Bion asks himself (and the reader), What are you going to do with these contradictory thoughts? (p. 67). He asks this question because he has to be able to think every thought – even the thought that negates everything that has led up to it.

Bion's thinking in this paragraph seems to follow the shape of a dream. His mental meanderings reflect valuable, unconstrained primary-process thinking, but, as in a dream, this is interwoven with secondary-process thinking. I believe that the paragraph contains a valuable idea that Bion left for others to develop: that all dreams are visual hallucinations in sleep and therefore reflect the unthought, unthinkable residue of unconscious thinking.

VII

Dreams as Works in Progress and Works in Stasis

Based on my clinical work with patients' dreams, it seems to me fruitful to combine Bion's two ways of viewing dreams that I have just discussed. From that binocular perspective, dreams contain (1) elements on which some psychological work has been done, and (2) elements on which no work has been accomplished. Even in dreams that yield a great deal of self-understanding, there are undreamt parts.[5] It is as if in dreams we are in conversation with ourselves, and much is left unsayable and unthinkable. The unthought and unthinkable parts of the dream reflect the fact that we are evading those truths that we most fear.

Much has been said about patients who bring dreams to the analyst composed of emotional experiences that are too disturbing for them to deal with on their own, and how we – the analytic pair – continue dreaming the disturbing emotional experience together. As an analyst, I am, of course, interested in the parts of a patient's dream that the patient has already substantially dreamt, i.e., the parts in which the emotional work has already been done. But, as Bion said, "What you know, you know – we needn't bother with that. We have to deal with all that we don't know" (Bion, 1987, p. 158). In other words, in my work, I am at least as interested in the undreamt parts of the patient's dreams – the unthinkable, unverbalizable, uninterpretable parts – the analysis of which may extend the patient's self-understanding to include an awareness of the "unthinkable." I am very interested in what the patient is trying to dream but cannot dream – the hallucinatory elements in dreams. Working with the hallucinatory aspect of dreams usually involves attending to my reverie states and other sensory responses that I experience while the patient is telling me his dream. In this way I help the patient continue (or begin) dreaming the undreamt portions of his dream.

Although I find that every dream contains hallucinatory elements, some are more obvious than others, and some are so subtle that I do not easily recognize them or miss them altogether. Nightmares are a form of incomplete dreaming "disrupted at a point where the individual's capacity for generating dream-thoughts and dreaming . . . is overwhelmed" (Ogden, 2004, p. 5). In nightmares, patients have done the work up to the point that they become so frightened by the dream-thought that they awaken in a state of fear requiring, "the mind of another person – 'one acquainted with the night' – to help [them] dream the yet to be dreamt aspect of [the] nightmare" (Ogden, 2004, p. 5).

Almost every night "for as long as I can remember," Mr. T, a Viet Nam veteran, experienced the same dream, which mirrored his time in Viet Nam as the "shooter" on a gunboat patrolling the Mekong River on midnight watch. He described his experience on the gunboat as having been one of chronic terror – of fearing for his life – and of witnessing many of his friends being "gunned down" by snipers "who kept popping up out of nowhere from underground bunkers on the river bank." Mr. T told me with a hint of anxious pride that since returning from "Nam" he is "always on guard – to the point of being hyper-vigilant" when he is awake and while he sleeps. He described his sleep pattern as erratic: he sleeps for a short period of time; he awakes in a startle in response to the slightest sound; and he checks out his surroundings ("secures the perimeter") and attempts to get back to sleep.

Each night his dreams are the same except for minor changes. He introduced the dream the first time by saying, "I had this weird dream, but I can't see how it fits in with all we've been talking about, but maybe you can help me." In the dream, his rifle is old and rusty, "like a Springfield rifle someone dug up from World War I," and the gunboat does not have its usual camouflage netting and olive drab paint. As he nervously scans the riverbank, the Vietcong start "popping up" as he desperately tries to load bullets (the wrong caliber) into the chamber of his rusty rifle. The rifle jams, and he feels paralyzed with terror, unable to shoot and unable to eject the jammed rounds; he awakes in a panic.

Mr. T. was telling me that he did not know how to think – "I can't see how it fits" [like his bullets] and wanted me to help him dream the dream from the point where he was "paralyzed." In this post-traumatic nightmare, little psychological work got done, but Mr. T kept returning to "work" on it. He was unable to shift his psychological state to a dreaming state because to do so would be to "let his guard down." This terror kept him in a continuous action mode of concentrated attention and problem solving, but it kept him from dreaming/thinking in the analysis, either on his own or with me.

If Mr. T were to allow himself to dream the dream, he would think and feel the overwhelming impact of the images and risk becoming psychotic. But by repeating the old (familiar) images, little or no psychological work was achieved, which for him at the time was by far the best of the alternatives. Mr. T was trying to control the scene on the river in all of its horror – trying to get rid of a terrifying state of "not know-ing" by evacuation, and thereby not dreaming the experience. And yet, the images "kept popping up." The psychic reality was so disturbing that it was transformed into something like a visual hallucination. Thinking stopped, and actions took over – as if saving his life depended on keeping his sights (hallucinatorially) on the enemy and not dreaming/not knowing. Mr. T's hallucinatory thinking did not allow him to learn from experience – it just allowed him briefly to get away from a psychological experi-ence that he feared would be overwhelming.

Some time later, Mr. T started a session by saying, "I woke up today and felt good – surprising because I had horrible dreams. Usually dreams leave me in a state of mind that is scary [having no mind to dream]. But this time it felt akin to having seen a good movie." In his reaction to his dreams, Mr. T was expressing a common belief: that after having dreams that are frightening, we wake up disturbed. It is not the dream itself – nor those parts of a dream that we have been able to dream – that is disturbing. Rather, it is the parts of dreams that we are not able to dream on our own (the hallucinatory parts) that are the most frightening because they are too emotionally overwhelming. I said to Mr. T, "Your dream seems to be pointing out something very different: when you are not able to dream, you awake feeling frightened."

Dreams other than nightmares also contain clear hallucinatory elements. Halluci-natory elements could be reflected in other ways such as by an absence of associations, psychotic non-thinking, or somatic responses on my part or on the patient's part.

When we are with a patient and do not want to admit to ourselves that we have no associations to a dream, we can always come up with something. In writing this chapter, it would be impossible for me to present a dream to which neither the patient nor I had any associations without the reader feeling that the patient and I had simply failed to recognize meaningful, emotion-laden elements. The reader necessarily will have associations as he or she would to a Rorschach card, but that does not mean that the card or the dream is communicating something to him.

Another encounter with the hallucinatory elements of dreaming occurred in my work with Mrs. B. In this example, I use the term *dreaming* in its broadest sense of being able to do unconscious psychological work, which is not necessarily visually representational in form.

Most of my analytic work with Mrs. B focused on her responses to her teenage son's dying in a car accident while he was traveling to compete in a swim meet. She was tormented by self-blame which her former husband cruelly played upon by say-ing, "You allowed the boy to drive in the middle of a rainstorm." She felt that her life had stopped when her son died, as if she "had fallen into a deep dark hole and died alongside him." She developed panic attacks and carried a paper bag into which she breathed during an attack.

In our sessions, she held herself perfectly still [stiff] and tightly composed on the couch. Her few responses to my comments came only after long silences. When she did respond, she barely moved her lips as she spoke. As I watched Mrs. B lying stiffly on the couch, I had the image of a corpse I had seen on display prior to cremation on the banks of the Ganges River. She told me she felt nothing, she had no existence without her son, her future was gone, her life was over.

Mrs. B. experienced me as blaming her for her son's death as her husband did – and as she herself did. Although she came to analysis with an emotional problem to be solved, she felt the only solution was "for you to bring him back from the dead – I want him back." She had no desire to be alive without him. Very concretely, Mrs. B was coming to me to give her back her son. She did not want to engage in thinking or analysis – what good would that do her in her effort to retrieve her son? I could feel how awful it was for her to have lost her son, and wished I could bring him back to her.

Mrs. B was unable to use my interventions, which led me to doubt myself as an analyst. My interventions contained a defensive, "overly empathic" "knowing" and "understanding." I was responding in ways that were not only un-analytical but mechanical that had served to protect me against my own feelings of deadness and ineffectiveness.

At this point in our work, the few dreams she reported contained undifferentiated figures, in which she changed into her son and back again into herself. In so doing, she magically carried her son back from the dead. She could not dream the death of her son. I entered into that inability to dream – instead, I was slipping into wishes for a magical reincarnation. [Reverie is a waking form of thinking/dreaming, and magical thinking is a form of psychotic reverie – a dream that is not a dream.]

After some time my emotional experience during our sessions began to include dissociated sensory and somatic experiences. I found myself rubbing my fingertips because they were cold and tingling, as if going numb. As I looked at my hands, I felt confused. Was I cold, were my fingertips losing sensation? Were they *my* fingertips? Later, I understood my somatic response as withdrawal into a psychotic state lacking depth of thought, emotion, and the capacity for self-reflection – a thorough preoccupation with numb fingertips that did not feel like my own. Disconnected from my body, I was unable to make analytic use of my bodily sensations.

On another occasion, when I met with Mrs. B in the waiting room, my stomach felt upset and was gurgling (I was not experiencing hunger), and I tightened my abdominal muscles to quiet my stomach. [I was trying not to wake her or myself from the deadness she/we continued to feel.]

At some point during this period of the analysis, I understood my thoughts to her magical wish for me to "bring her son back from the dead" as connected to my earlier reverie of the Ganges River – and the Hindu (magical) belief that if one is cremated during the correct phase of the lunar cycle, through incarnation, one will magically come back from the dead – i.e., be reborn.

I also understood my bodily reactions as an attempt to hold and digest for her what was unholdable and undigestable, and, for the time being, undreamable. With this awareness, I was able to release the tension in my abdominal muscles and let go of my "omnipotent control." I began to feel something beyond the "knowing" and "understanding" responses I had felt earlier. I experienced a new awareness, a bodily sensation of my own that I expressed through my tone of voice. In this way, I was on the threshold of bringing together the sensory and the real – the beta elements and the alpha function – to be used for thinking. I was able to help the patient to (or perhaps more accurately, to begin) dream what had been undreamable – to recognize and acknowledge that her son was separate from her and dead.

Shortly after this experience, in a dream that felt somewhat different from the others, Mrs. B dreamt that she was swimming underwater and only the bubbles from her breathing were surfacing. She followed the bubbles to the surface and took a deep breath. As the dream continued, her son appeared in the center of an otherwise-empty stage. She approached him from the audience and felt herself hugging him. "I actually felt his physical presence – could smell his essence and feel the softness of his skin against mine." This physical sensation of holding her son stayed with her when she awoke, and provided her with a way to begin to live with the loss – to feel not only a deep sadness but also a sense of calm. By making the loss physically real, she was able to complete (as much as possible) putting her son to rest, and "resurfacing" in her life, reclaiming her own life separate from her son but with a place for him. Moving beyond the limitations of magical non-thinking, she achieved the capacity to dream.

In retrospect, my initial response to Mrs. B (i.e., superficially "understanding" and "knowing") involved a wish to offer containment, an unconscious desire to magically bring back her son. Rather than dreaming about what she could not dream, I took in what she evacuated into me and let it "stagnate" further (in the form of my magical thinking).

Only when I became aware of my omnipotent wish to bring back her son, and could be aware of my bodily sensations as my own, was I able to move beyond the place where she could dream no further on her own (and, in important ways, was not able to dream at all). What began as a delusion developed into reveries and into forms of waking dreaming that allowed me to think and dream with her. This was a new creation that was entirely different from hallucinatory experience; what had started as a delusion developed into reveries that allowed me to think and dream with Mrs. B.

Summary

Freud believes dreaming does not inform or resolve conflicted emotional experience for the dreamer on his or her own; rather, dreams are fully interpretable and understandable only by the analyst, who puts the repressed meaning (latent content) of the dream into words for the patient. The analyst, not the patient, does the work of interpreting the dream by connecting latent content to manifest content, thereby giving the dream verbally symbolized meaning. The patient then works with the analyst's interpretations of the dream.

Dreaming, for Bion, is the primary psychoanalytic function of the mind. It involves the pursuit of truth by means of thinking and feeling; the mind is developed through dreaming as we strive to discover what is true to our experience. Bion's "work of dreaming" allows conscious lived emotional experience to become available to the unconscious for dreaming, so that a person may better look at different ideas about, or solutions to, an emotional problem. The patient's capacity for alpha function underlies his ability to process raw emotional experience, that is, to make it meaningful and available for unconscious psychological work.

Extending Bion's ideas, I have suggested that dreams are psychological works in progress and yet regularly contain elements that the dreamer has been unable to dream because of the disturbing nature of the emotional experience. Bion believes that there is a psychotic and non-psychotic part of every personality; I am suggesting that there is a psychotic and non-psychotic part of every dream. The non-psychotic part tells us what the patient knows (is able to think or begin to think), while the psychotic part presents to us what the patient is unable to think. The latter is the part of the dream that the patient is unable to dream and constitutes something akin to a visual hallucination in sleep. The analytic work with this part of the dream involves both analyst and patient developing the capacity to dream (that is, to unconsciously process) the previously undreamt part of the dream.

Notes

1   Historically, dreams were considered part of mythology. They were used to foretell the future through the dream interpreter and were viewed as "a formidable or hostile manifestation by higher powers, daemonic and divine" (Freud, 1900/1953b, p. 633). "[T]here may have been a time when a campaign without dream interpreters seemed as impossible as one without air-reconnaissance seems to-day. When Alexander the Great started on his conquests, his train included the most famous dream interpreters" (Freud, 1916/1961a, pp. 85–86).
2   The topographic model is an archaeological metaphor cast in terms of the unconscious, preconscious, and conscious "levels" of the mind, and the structural model is a metaphor of a "group" consisting of the id, ego, and superego.
3   "There is, in fact, no better analogy for repression, by which something in the mind is at once made inaccessible and preserved, than burial of the sort to which Pompeii fell a victim and from which it could emerge once more through the work of spades" (Freud, 1906/1959, p. 40). The repressed stays intact; no growth occurs without an analyst to do the work of interpretation.
4   With the concept of "dream-work alpha" (which is synonymous with what he later called alpha function), Bion added dream activity occurring in a waking state to Freud's dreaming while asleep.
5   When I say "unable to dream," I am not talking about that ultimate mystery in ourselves that cannot be put into visual images or dream-thoughts, that can never be brought into our experience, and always remains unknown, which Bion (1970) refers to as "O" (see Grotstein, 2000).

References

Bion, W. R. (1962). *Learning from experience*. Basic Books.
Bion, W. R. (1967). A theory of thinking. In *Second thoughts*. Aronson.
Bion, W. R. (1970). *Attention and interpretation*. Karnac Books.
Bion, W. R. (1980a). Preface. In F. Bion (Ed.), *Bion in New York and São Paulo*. Clunie Press.
Bion, W. R. (1980b). *Bion in New York and São Paulo* (F. Bion, Ed.). Clunie Press.

Bion, W. R. (1987). *Clinical seminars and other works*. Karnac Books.

Bion, W. R. (1992). *Cogitations*. Karnac Books.

De M'Uzan, M. (1984). Slaves of quantity. *Psychoanalytic Quarterly, 72*, 711–725.

Freud, S. (1953a). *The interpretation of dreams*. In J. Strachey (Ed. & Trans.), Standard edition of the complete psychological works of Sigmund Freud (Vol. 4, pp. 1–338). Hogarth Press. (Original work published 1900)

Freud, S. (1953b). *The interpretation of dreams*. In J. Strachey (Ed. & Trans.), Standard edition of the complete psychological works of Sigmund Freud (Vol. 5, pp. 339–723). Hogarth Press. (Original work published 1900)

Freud, S. (1957). *On the history of the psycho-analytic movement*. Papers on metapsychology and other works. In J. Strachey (Ed. & Trans.), Standard edition of the complete psychological works of Sigmund Freud (Vol. 14, pp. 3–359). Hogarth Press. (Original work published in 1915)

Freud, S. (1958). *The case of Shreber*. In J. Strachey (Ed. & Trans.), Standard edition of the complete psychological works of Sigmund Freud (Vol. 12, pp.3–361). Hogarth Press. (Original work published 1911)

Freud, S. (1959). Jensen's Gradiva and other works. In J. Strachey (Ed. & Trans.), Standard edition of the complete psychological works of Sigmund Freud (Vol. 9, pp. 3–95). Hogarth Press. (Original work published 1906-1908).

Freud, S. (1961a). *Introductory lectures on psycho-analysis*. In J. Strachey (Ed. & Trans.), Standard edition of the complete psychological works of Sigmund Freud (Vol. 15, pp. 3–483). Hogarth Press. (Original work published 1916)

Freud, S. (1961b). *The ego and the id*. In J. Strachey (Ed. & Trans.), Standard edition of the complete psychological works of Sigmund Freud (Vol. 19, pp. 3–309). Hogarth Press. (Original work published 1923)

Freud, S. (1964a). New introductory lectures on psychoanalysis. In J. Strachey (Ed. & Trans.), *Standard edition of the complete psychological works of Sigmund Freud* (Vol. 22). Hogarth Press. (Original work published 1933)

Freud, S. (1964b). Revision of the theory of dreams. In J. Strachey (Ed. & Trans.), *Standard edition of the complete psychological works of Sigmund Freud* (Vol. 22, pp. 7–30). Hogarth Press. (Original work published 1933)

Grotstein, J. S. (2000). *Who is the dreamer who dreams the dream?* Analytic Press.

Grotstein, J. S. (2002). "We are such stuff as dreams are made on": Annotations on dreams and dreaming in Bion's works. In C. Neri, M. Pines, & R. Friedman (Eds.), *Dreams in group psychotherapy: Theory and technique*. Jessica Kingsley.

Grotstein, J. S. (2007). *A beam of intense darkness*. Karnac Books.

McDougall, J. (1984). The "dis-affected" patient: Reflections on affect pathology. *Psychoanalytic Quarterly, 53*, 386–409.

Meltzer, D. (1983). *Dream-life: A re-examination of the psychoanalytical theory and technique*. Clunie Press.

Nietzsche, F. (n.d.). Unnamed source. Cited in M. Ondaatje. (2007). *Divisadero*. Knopf.

Ogden, T. H. (2004). On holding and containing, being and dreaming. *International Journal of Psychoanalysis, 85*, 1349–1364.

Ogden, T. H. (2005). *This art of psychoanalysis: Dreaming undreamt dreams and interrupted cries*. London: Routledge. New Library of Psychoanalysis.

Ogden, T. H. (2007). On talking as dreaming. *International Journal of Psychoanalysis, 88*, 575–589.

Schneider, J. A. (2003a). Janus-faced resilience in the analysis of a severely traumatized patient. *Psychoanalytic Review, 90*(6), 869–887.

Schneider, J. A. (2003b). Working with pathological and healthy forms of splitting: A case study. *Bulletin of the Menninger Clinic, 67*(1), 32–49.

Schneider, J. A. (2005a). Experiences in K and –K. *International Journal of Psychoanalysis, 86*(3), 825–839.

Schneider, J. A. (2005b). Reply to Dr. Alexander. *International Journal of Psychoanalysis, 86*(5), 1479.

Schneider, J. A. (2005c). Dreaming the truth of experience: "Heaven." *Psychoanalytic Review, 92*(5), 777–785.

Tustin, F. (1982) *Autistic states in children*. Routledge and Kegan Paul.

Waldhorn, H. F. (Reporter) (1967). The place of the dream in clinical psychoanalysis. In *Monograph series of the Kris study group*. Psychoanalytic Institute.

3

Bion's Thinking About Groups

A Study of Influence and Originality

How to describe the interplay between mind and body has long been a challenge for psychoanalytic theorists. In this chapter, I will discuss what I believe to be one of Bion's least-acknowledged contributions to psychoanalytic theory: his study of the relationship between the mind of the individual (the ability to think), the mentalities of groups of which the individual is a member, and the individual's bodily states. In his work on these three aspects of human experience, he demonstrates the way in which the interaction among them has a powerful influence on the health (or illness) of the individual and the maturation of the psyche-soma (Bion, 1978, 1991).

I will go on to extend Bion's ideas on this interaction among the thinking of the individual, group mentality, and the psyche-soma to include my own conception of the way in which group mentality is surprisingly recognizable in the analysis of individuals and serves as a constant backdrop to personal experience, integral to the very foundation of a sense of self. In the tradition of Bion, I believe that we are always under the influence of the group – that the phantasies of the groups in which we are members are ever present, whether we are with a group, with another person, or by ourselves.

More than 60 years ago, Bion published his earliest essays between 1943 and 1951 in a book titled *Experiences in Groups* (1961). In this early work, Bion used groups as laboratories in which to explore his understanding of the mind-body connection. The first paper in this series of essays, "Pre-View: Intra-Group Tensions in Therapy" (Bion, 1961), written in collaboration with John Rickman, discusses a novel form of "leaderless" group therapy that Bion and Rickman developed at the military facility where Bion was director of a rehabilitation center during World War II. The paper's subtitle, "Their Study as the Task of the Group," suggests to me that Bion was "not concerned to give individual treatment in public" (Bion, 1961, p. 80) – that is, he was not exploring a therapeutic approach but was primarily interested in investigating the group as an entity. "The group was essential to myself because I wished to have a group to study" (p. 54). Based on insights early in his career about how individuals think within groups, Bion posited a social instinct – groupishness (Bion, 1961)[1] and began developing his theory of thinking.

The difficulty posed by Bion's concept of groupishness – as with Freud's concept of the sexual instinct and Klein's notion of the death instinct – is the question of how

DOI:10.4324/9781003384601-3

the mind goes about solving problems presented by instinctual (bodily) pressure. With groupishness, the mind must wrestle with the combination of its inborn need to be a member of groups and its need to know the truth of its experience. Human beings are conflicted between the pull of their individual thoughts and the pull of their instinctual groupishness (i.e., their collective identity and their need to be of one mind with the group).

With the exception of his concept of groupishness, which I will discuss later in this chapter, Bion does not depart much from Freud's structural model or the inherent tensions of id, ego, and superego (Freud, 1930/1962; see also Lacan, 1966). Bion proposed that the mind develops in response to the conflict inherent in being both a group member and a person with thoughts of his own.

When Bion speaks of the mind, he is referring to the interrelated workings of the mind and body and its inherent psychic conflict; and when he speaks of thoughts, he is referring to thoughts and feelings (including emotions – the bodily components of feelings). "The individual has to live in his own body, and his body has to put up with a mind living in it" (Bion, 2005, p. 10).

Here Bion addresses the age-old problem of how an individual's mind and body respond and contribute to group pressures that conflict with the individual's thinking – anxieties that press to co-mingle the boundaries minding the body and bodying the mind – and how this conflict is given meaning. Based on his understanding of this tension, Bion developed a comprehensive theory of thinking that relates bodily sensations to thought. He proposed that the development of thinking results from using our minds to solve emotional problems and to deal with thoughts (alpha elements) that are generated in response to intimate emotional experience:

> The development of thoughts . . . require[s] an apparatus to cope with them . . . [an] apparatus that I shall provisionally call thinking . . .. This differs from any theory of thought as a product of thinking, in that thinking is a development forced on the psyche by the pressure of thoughts and not the other way around.
>
> (Bion, 1965, pp. 110–111)

Bion writes that "sense impressions [beta elements] related to emotional experience" (1962, p. 17) are converted to alpha elements (which can be linked in the process of thinking). He goes on to say, "Beta elements [are] a way of talking about matters which are not thought at all; alpha-elements are a way of talking about elements which, hypothetically, are supposed to be part of thought" (1990, p. 41). Bion distinguishes between "primitive thinking" as a precursor for the development of thought, and "thinking required for the use of thoughts" (1963, p. 35) once thoughts are formed. This presupposes that thinking is a multistep process that begins before awareness or perception, at a protomental (bodily, sensory) level.

To expand upon what I said earlier, I will discuss in this chapter how Bion, in his work on groups, takes on a problem that he addresses nowhere else in his vast body of work: the interplay of group mentality, individuality of thought, and the pressures of bodily instinct (in this case, the social instinct of groupishness). I will describe how

Bion used the contributions of Freud, Trotter, and Klein to formulate his ideas about how humans think, feel, and behave in groups, as well as his original contributions to the study of groups. Bion does not refute those whom he followed; instead, he shows how each of them presents a valid perspective and then discusses how their theories are consistent with and contribute to his encompassing theory of thinking.[2]

For clarity of exposition, I have divided the body of this chapter into three main parts: "Influence," "Originality," and "Experiencing in Groups."

I – Influence

Freud's Influence on Bion's Thinking About Groups

In his early papers, Bion generously refers to his theory of groups as an extension of Freud's theory: "I am impressed, as a practicing psychoanalyst, by the fact that the psychoanalytic approach through the individual, and the approach these papers describe through the group, are dealing with different facets of the same phenomena" (1961, p. 8).

Bion notes that after Freud's initial observations on the individual yielded little insight, he began analyzing the transference in the analytic dyad to gain access to the patient's unconscious thoughts, feelings, fantasies, and so on:

> Before Freud . . . the individual was considered to be an intelligible field of study, but it was when Freud began to seek a solution in the relationship between two people, in study of the transference, that he found what was the intelligible field of study for at least some of the problems that the neurotic patient poses.
>
> (Bion, 1961, p. 104)

Bion (1961) expanded this "intelligible field of study" to include groups, pointing out that the individual has characteristics whose significance cannot be understood unless it is acknowledged that the individual is a herd animal interacting with other humans. The study of groups was important to Bion because it allowed access to observations of an individual psyche otherwise unavailable (1961). He proposed that studying groupishness does not require that "number[s] of people are collected together in one place at one time" (p. 168). In fact, a group has "no significance for the production of group phenomena" (p. 168). In this proposition, Bion was making a major paradigm shift: he emphasized that group dynamics are inherent in individuals, and that they continue to develop in individuals even though they are most evident when individuals are together in groups. Bion believed, contrary to Freud (1921/1961b, 1922/1961a), that the herd instinct is not a phenomenon overlaying mental life: "In my view, no new instinct is brought into play – it is always in play" (Bion, 1961, p. 131). "The individual is, and always has been, a member of a group" (p. 168).

This differed dramatically from Freud's (1921/1961b) thinking. Freud imported his theory of individual analysis into his thinking about groups based on his structural model (1923/1961c), while Bion imported ideas derived from groups and the herd mentality into his understanding of the individual mind. Bion expanded Freud's and Trotter's ideas about groups to develop his own integrated theory of how we think as individuals who are never outside the influence of the mentalities of the groups to which we belong. Freud explicitly rejected the idea of a herd instinct, using the workings of suggestion and libido to explain group phenomena.

To understand how the mind works, Bion introduced a novel method of observation that goes beyond Freud's "explanatory" model of psychoanalysis. Basically, Bion (1961) proposed that psychoanalysts use their "mental microscope" (p. 49) to hold multiple points of view at the same time – each providing information from its own vantage point while influencing the others. The instrument of observation (thinking) that adjusts in order to "illume" one's observations with a "rudimentary binocular vision" (1961, p. 8) offers points of view that are continuously changing while overlapping, thus informing and transforming each other from multiple vantage points simultaneously. This is evidenced in Bion's models of the dialectical interplay between the conscious and unconscious mind, the psychotic and nonpsychotic parts of the personality, and primary- and secondary-process thinking.

Bion reconceived many of Freud's mental constructs (for example, the relationship between the conscious and unconscious mind), proposing instead that we are aware of and have access to both poles of these dichotomies simultaneously. Bion focused on multiple realities as part of the reality principle – relying on observation of facts from multiple vertices to get to the selected fact by using a scientific approach of investigation, as well as personal creativity and intuition. When we extend Bion's conception of the simultaneity of multiple vertices to the analytic relationship, both the patient's and analyst's state of mind are seen as contributing to the creation of a mind capable of thinking and generating meaning.

Freud's paternalistic view that observations are filtered through the lens of the analyst as "chief" evidences his belief in the centrality of the analyst's position in the therapeutic relationship – whereas Bion develops the view that, in analysis, "it takes two people to think" (Ogden & Ogden, 2013, p. 25), with each member of the dyad thinking with the other and having a significant effect on the other's defenses and emotions.

Trotter's Influence on Bion's Thinking About Groups

Perhaps the person who most influenced Bion's thinking about groups was Wilfred Trotter. In her introduction to Bion's autobiographical essay, Francesca Bion (1985) states that there were two outstanding men who "played a very great part in his [Bion's] intellectual development" (p. 7). One was H. J. Patton, an authority on Kant's philosophy with whom Bion studied when he was an undergraduate at Oxford; and the other was Wilfred Trotter, his surgical chief when Bion was a medical student at University College Hospital in London. It can be said that Bion owed much of his theoretical thinking to Trotter, whom he looked to as a mentor and father figure.

Trotter is best known in medical circles as an outstanding surgeon, and in socio-psychoanalytic circles for having conceived of the herd instinct (Trotter, 1916/2005). Although not well acknowledged for his contributions to psychoanalysis, Trotter influenced psychoanalytic thought through his friend Ernest Jones. It was Trotter who developed the concept of rationalization, which, at Trotter's instigation, Jones presented at the First International Congress at Salzburg in 1908. Trotter introduced Jones to Freud, and it was Trotter who attended to Freud when Freud was near death (Jones, 1940; Maddox, 2006).

Trotter's (1916/2005) work on groups preceded Freud's 1921 paper on group psychology. Trotter, however, did not provide a theoretical framework or observational data with which to address the problem of how, in human beings, the herd instinct becomes a mental phenomenon as a result of the reflective I or self that herd animals are not capable of generating (Schneider, 2009).

Trotter's ideas about the herd instinct were seminal to Bion's (1961) thinking about groups, and by extension to all of Bion's theoretical contributions about how the mind works.[3] Bion was in agreement with Trotter's contention that gregariousness is the strongest urge in human beings:

> The individual has an even more dangerous problem to solve [than sexuality] in the operation of his aggressive impulses, which . . . may impose on him the need to fight for his group with the essential possibility of death, while it also imposes on him the need for action in the interests of his survival.
>
> (Bion, 1992, pp. 105–106)

Trotter (1916/2005) distinguished between "three primitive instincts" (p. 47) – survival, sexual pairing, and feeding – that are activated by the individual and obey the pleasure principle, and what he called the "fourth instinct of gregariousness" (p. 47), which is activated by the group and controlled by a power outside the body.

> The fourth instinct . . . exercises a controlling power on the individual from without . . . and may actually be unpleasant, and so be resisted from the individual side and yet be forced instinctively into execution. The instinctive act seems to have been too much associated in current thought [i.e., in Freud's pleasure principle] with the idea of yielding to an impulse irresistibly pleasant to the body. [p. 48; italics added] . . .. The others automatically fall into the background.
>
> (Trotter, 1916/2005, p. 47)

Extending Trotter's ideas, it seems that the instinctual social force is an internal state at birth activated from outside the body, which eventually encompasses the entirety of our past and present group experiences.

Bion (1992) concurred with Trotter regarding the primacy of gregariousness over sexual and aggressive instincts: "The patient's socialism menaces his primacy as an individual, and the group demands of him subordination to aims lying outside his personality" (p. 105) – but the group is nonetheless necessary for his sanity and psychological growth.

In proposing the herd instinct, Trotter gives gregariousness biological significance as a bodily instinct, which in Bion's theory is transformed into a psychological trait (groupishness). Bion agreed with Trotter's (1916/2005) assessment that ordinary psychology is dealing with the two fields – the social and the individual – which are . . . absolutely continuous . . .. All human psychology . . . must be the psychology of associated man, since man as a solitary animal is unknown to us, and every individual must present the characteristic reactions of the social animal (p. 12).

That man is also necessarily a sociopolitical animal is a human condition recognized as early in human civilization as Aristotle's time: "Aristotle said man is a political animal; for a man to lead a full life, the group is essential . . . to the fulfillment of a man's life . . . as essential . . . as . . . activities of economics and war" (Bion, 1961, pp. 53–54). Furthermore:

> The inescapable bestiality of the human animal is the quality from which our cherished and admired characteristics spring. "Man is a political animal" means that he has the mental counterpart of the physical characteristics of a herd animal. As psychoanalysts, we are concerned with the mental counterpart of such physical characteristics as can be discerned in the individual when in semi-isolation from his group, but closely involved in a situation likely to stimulate his "pair" characteristics.
> (Bion, 1970, pp. 65–66)

Here, it seems to me, the important idea is that the influence of the group continues regardless of our awareness or intent – whether we are surrounded by others, by ourselves, or in an analytic dyad. Trotter believed humans are so dominated by the herd instinct that they develop an internal representation of the herd so they can travel and live alone when necessary. Echoing Trotter, Bion (1961) asks, "How do we know when the group begins, or for that matter when it ends?" (p. 88). He responds by saying that we humans are never "not in the group," even when we are alone. "No individual, however isolated in time and space, can be regarded as outside a group or lacking in active manifestations of group psychology" (1961, p. 132). "The group, in the sense of a collection of people in a room, adds nothing to the individual or the aggregate of individuals – it merely reveals something that is not otherwise visible" (p. 340).

Like Trotter, Bion believed humans always carry the herd's internal representation, and are therefore suggestible. Trotter (1916/2005) wrote: "Man is not . . . suggestible in fits and starts, not merely in panics and in mobs, under hypnosis, and so forth, but [is] *always, everywhere, and under any circumstances* . . . identified with the voice of the herd" (p. 33, italics added).

In this regard, Bion differed from Freud (1921/1961b), who felt that group members align with the leader in a trance-like way due to their heightened suggestibility in the presence of the leader, replacing their own superego with that of the leader as a result of their identification with him. Suggestibility for Bion, by contrast, is an inherent state that is automatic.

Bion proposed that human beings share a belief system that takes on evolutionary importance. They find it almost impossible to hold ideas that conflict with the group mentality, subordinating their individual beliefs and taking as fact what are really shared belief systems that resist and repel contradictory knowledge. He wrote,

"The natural psychological habitat is a group animal at war not simply with the group, but with himself for being a group animal" (1961, p. 131) – and we have the choice of either accepting the thinking of the group or adding our own ideas.

Trotter contends that gregariousness enhances our chances for survival and evolution, favoring the survival of the herd over the individual. Bion (1992) echoes Trotter's belief:

> In his relationship with the group, the individual's welfare is secondary to the survival of the group. Darwin's theory of the survival of the fittest needs to be replaced by a theory of the survival of the fittest to survive in a group [as an individual].
>
> (pp. 29–30)

Klein's Influence on Bion's Thinking About Groups

At one point, Bion linked his theory of groups to Melanie Klein's (1946/1952) psychoanalytic concepts. The final chapter of *Experiences in Groups* (Bion, 1961) is dedicated to her. In the introduction to that chapter, Bion stated:

> My present work . . . convinces me of the central importance of the Kleinian theories of projective identification and the interplay between the paranoid-schizoid and depressive positions . . .. Without the aid of these two sets of theories, I doubt the possibility of any advance in the study of group phenomena.
>
> (p. 8)

He included in his thinking Klein's "theories of internal objects, projective identification, and failure of symbol formation" (Bion, 1952, p. 247). Bion's theory of groups builds on her idea that an individual's psychotic anxieties, generated in the context of first encounters with the object (mother/breast), are reactivated when the individual attempts to make contact with members of a group.

As well as deepening our understanding of many of the concepts introduced by Klein, Bion greatly extended her theory. For instance, he transformed the concept of projective identification (which he thought "played an important role in groups" (1961, p. 149) from an intrapsychic mechanism of defense to a psychological/interpersonal process by which two individuals think together. In Bion's conception of projective identification, the analyst experiences himself in accord with the feelings projected into him by the patient and, in response to interpersonal pressure, finds himself "playing a part . . . in somebody else's phantasy" (p. 149). The patient influences the analyst in such a way that he suffers "a temporary loss of insight" (p. 149).

Bion (1962, 1963) expanded projective identification into a concept of communicativeness, extending it to include a very primitive form of thinking, allowing the patient "to investigate his own feelings in a personality powerful enough to contain them" (Bion, 1959, p. 314). He elaborates this when he states, "In its origin, communication is effected by realistic projective identification" (1967, p. 118).

Bion continued to develop his own thinking, even when his ideas seemed to alter Klein's. He did not let the influence of others dictate his process of creating meaning. At every point in his career, Bion refused to align himself with a particular psychoanalytic school of thought. "More than one patient has said my technique is not Kleinian. I think there is substance in this" (Bion, 1992, p. 166).

II – Originality

Having discussed the influences of Freud, Klein, and Trotter on Bion's thinking about groups, I will now turn to what I see as original to Bion's contribution to a psychoanalytic theory of thinking that encompasses both individual and group life. I will divide this discussion of Bion's contribution into four subsections, each of which deals with different aspects of his thinking – or perhaps it would be more accurate to say that these are different vertices from which to view his thinking: Bion's conception of basic assumption groups, of work groups, of the protomental matrix, and of the analytic dyad.

Bion's Basic Assumption Groups

Bion (1961) transformed Trotter's biological herd instinct into elements of "group mentality" (p. 60) that he called "basic assumption groups" (p. 153). These shared unconscious beliefs are nonthinking responses with the strength of instincts, which exist as primitive protomental states and can preempt thinking and override observations. The basic assumptions stem from the gregarious instinct, which aligns group members to share their beliefs, emotions, and phantasies, demonstrating a "readiness to combine . . . that is more analogous to tropism in plants than to purposive behavior" (Bion, 1961, pp. 116–117).

Bion (1961) referred to the tendency for humans to group together as a "valency" – that is, "a spontaneous unconscious formation of the gregariousness quality in the personality of man" (p. 170). "[There is] no valency only by ceasing to be . . . human" (p. 116). Thus, to be human is to be under the ever-present influence of the gregarious quality of the personality, and to have the capacity for "instantaneous combinations with other humans in an established pattern of behavior – the basic assumption" (Bion, 1961, p. 175).[4]

The three basic assumption elements are basic assumption dependency, basic assumption pairing, and basic assumption fight-flight. Bion explains how these "basic assumption mentalities" manifest in groups. In a basic assumption dependency group, the group members "think they need only wait for a single sustaining leader who will solve all their problems" (p. 82). In a basic assumption pairing group, the group members participate in the creativity of a pair of individuals to produce a savior or saving idea, providing "a Messiah, be it a person, idea, or Utopia" (p. 152). In a basic assumption fight-flight group, the group attacks or flees from any dangerous object or idea; that is, all group problems can be solved by fighting or taking flight from an enemy.

Closely related to the idea that humans operate on basic assumptions is Bion's belief that "there is a hatred of having to learn by experience . . ." (Bion, 1961, p. 89), which is very close, if not identical, to Trotter's (1916/2005) notion that people resist changing what is familiar and known to them. "Experience, as is shown by the whole history of man, is met by resistance, because it invariably encounters decisions based upon instinctive belief" (Trotter, 1916/2005, p. 35). Trotter and Bion concur that unless a new idea fits already understandable ideas, it disappears. "The mind likes a strange idea as little as the body likes a strange protein, and resists it with similar energy . . . . A new idea is the most quickly acting antigen known to science" (Trotter, 1941, p. 189).

Bion (1961) seems to suggest that to learn from experience, one must develop the capacity to think in the face of the immediacy of instinctual feelings. "What we've learned from history is that we do not learn from history," and humans have a "hatred of a process of development" (p. 89). In using such emphatic language, Bion seems to be concurring with Trotter's ideas about thinking and anti-thinking. This also echoes Freud's (1930/1962) idea that we rid the body of pressure by "killing off the instincts" (p. 79), so as not to be left with frustrating feelings.

Acting on the basic assumptions allows access to the affiliated work group mentality, which initially presents as beta elements (the raw sensory data), to be transformed into units of meaningful experience (alpha elements), which can then be linked in the process of thinking and symbolization in the work group. But given the near rapidity of the valence with which basic assumptions are combined, the emotional potential of the protomental gets evacuated as beta elements. In other words, beta elements maintain some of the valence of protomental elements and are expelled by the mind; "the mind is felt to operate as if it were a muscle" (Bion, 1965, p. 130).

> [Beta elements are] expelled as air in the lungs is expelled . . . the patient seems to feel that his mind is an expelling organ like a lung in act of expiration . . . the patient is using his eyes, and the mental counterpart for vision, as evacuatory musculature.
> (Bion, 1965, p. 131)

As an example of Bion's thinking from multiple vertices, I will conclude this subsection by presenting his discussion of co-operation:

> In the group the patient feels he must try to co-operate. He discovers that his capacity for co-operation is emotionally most vital in the basic group, and that, in the pursuit of objectives that do not easily lend themselves to the techniques of the basic group, his ability to co-operate is dependent on a kind of give-and-take that is achieved with great difficulty compared with the swift emotional response that comes of acquiescence in the emotions of the basic group.
> (1961, p. 90)

The rapidity of the "physical" response of co-operation both limits and is necessary for the ability to move to a form of co-operation involving the pursuit of truth and development. The work group comes together to act on the basic assumption, with the potential to transform itself into the affiliated work group.

Later on in his discussion, Bion presents an example in his own thinking of shifting from a basic assumption mentality to the work group mentality when he reconsiders his earlier thinking about co-operation:

> In trying to achieve precision of aim, I was really suffering . . . through dislike of the emotional quality in myself and in the group that is inherent in membership of the human group . . . This quality is a [certain] kind of capacity for co-operation with the group, but I propose from now on to reserve the word co-operation for conscious or unconscious working with the rest of the group in work; whereas for the capacity for spontaneous instinctive co-operation in the basic assumptions . . . I shall use the word "valency."
>
> (1961, p. 116 [italics added])

As can be seen, Bion considers the word co-operation from multiple vertices, including his internal emotional response to his experience in a group. Consequently, he revises his thinking to use the word co-operation only as evidenced in the work group where group members are engaged in "co-operations" (i.e., simultaneous operations). The co-operation resulting from our capacity for instantaneous combination with others is an automatic basic assumption he calls "valency." Only when cooperative action becomes part of the work group mentality can thinking occur. The reader can hear in Bion's comments how his thinking process allowed him to shift from the basic assumption mentality to the work group mentality.

Bion's Work Groups

As Bion (1961) conceives of it, the work group is a group mentality that exists in tension with the basic assumption groups because, unlike the primitive automaticity of basic assumptions, the work group mentality involves a cooperative endeavor to pursue a common purpose in accord with the reality principle. Basic assumption groups appear to be thinking by using previously validated thoughts that avoid thinking. The work group exists because of "the need to develop [thinking] rather than to rely on the efficacy of magic" (Bion, 1961), which can only occur by "the painful bringing together" (p. 128) of the primitive basic assumption mentality and the "sophisticated" (p. 96) work group mentality. This is a process that necessitates facing our most primitive fears – our unconscious psychotic states that hate development and rely on magical thinking to avoid the truth (Schneider, 2005a, 2005b, 2005c).

In his 1950 paper on groups, Bion introduces his critical idea of the central importance of knowing the truth, an idea that he fully develops 20 years later in *Attention and Interpretation* (1970), which was originally titled *Attention and Interpretation: A Scientific Approach to Insight in Psychoanalysis and Groups.*

> A group acting on basic assumptions would need neither organization nor a capacity for co-operation. It is only when a group begins to act on a basic assumption that difficulties arise. Action inevitably means contact with reality, and contact with

reality compels regard for truth; scientific method is imposed, and the evocation of the work group follows.

(Bion, 1961, pp. 170–171)

While the instinctual tendency in humans is to form groups, basic assumption groups stand in opposition to thinking and, at the same time, are essential to thinking. The work group can get to the truth only by questioning assumed truths and examining facts, leading to the development of ideas challenging to the self.

It is almost as if human beings were aware of the painful and often-fatal consequences of having to act without an adequate grasp of reality, and therefore were aware of the need for truth as a criterion in the evaluation of their findings (Bion, 1961, p. 100).

We are equipped with an unrealized drive to pursue the truth, and in spite of our group mentality, our thinking ultimately confronts reality, so that our work group mentality wins out. "The group and the individuals in it are hopelessly committed to a developmental procedure, no matter what might have been the case with our remote ancestors [Trotter's 'herd']" (Bion, 1961, pp. 89–90).

"I think one of the striking things about a group is that, despite the influence of the basic assumptions, it is the work group that triumphs in the long run" (1961, p. 135). To guard against basic assumption mentalities taking over the work group mentality, in large groups at the Tavistock Clinic, Bion was known to ask, "Would anyone give a home to a wild idea?" (Britton, 2010), as an invitation to consider individual thoughts felt to be out of step with those of the group.

The task of the work group is to learn from the process of facing magical wishes inherent in the group's basic assumption mentalities. While we need external work groups to develop our thinking, one could just as easily say we are cursed with the limitations on thinking inherent in being members of groups operating at the level of basic assumptions. Both are true. "Without basic assumption groups, there would be nothing for the work group to work on" (Ogden, 2011).

Bion believes that a work group mentality is always at risk of deteriorating into a basic assumption group mentality, or anti-thinking. Learning and innovation can take place only if the work group mentality is allowed to interact with and destabilize basic assumption mentalities, similar to the way paranoid-schizoid splitting productively destabilizes depressive position certainty and closure.

Bion's Undeveloped Postulate of the Protomental Matrix

A third conception of groups that reflects Bion's originality of thinking is his conception of a protomental matrix that is the origin of the individual's emotional states. In this matrix, which underlies all human experience, "physical and psychological or mental are undifferentiated . . .. It is from this matrix that emotions proper to the basic assumptions flow" (Bion, 1961, p. 102). In this way, Bion extends his model of the self, linking the physical body and the psyche. The protomental matrix is not experienced consciously or unconsciously; rather, it is a constant state – the psychophysical basis of all emotion and thought.

As Bion (1961) states, the protomental "transcends experience" (p. 101). "The emotional state precedes the basic assumption and follows certain proto-mental phenomena of which it is an expression" (p. 101).

When Bion refers to transcending experience, we might ask ourselves what else is there – how can we know something beyond our own experience? Perhaps something else arises from the herd mentality and forms a background state that is activated when individuals are in groups.

Bion's theory of the protomental matrix extends far beyond Freud's conception of how the mind interacts with the body to transform instincts into events that develop into psychic illness. For Freud, hysteria results from an unconscious psychological conflict in which the body is used for symbolic expression of experiences that are so psychically disturbing that they are relegated to the unconscious through repression. But Bion sees all illness as evolving from the protomental matrix. Protomental phenomena may become either physical states (e.g., blushing) or illnesses (e.g., tuberculosis) (Bion, 1961) without psychological registration, or they may become thoughts and emotional states (and good physical health).

The ascension of one of the basic assumptions means that the force and influence of the other two basic assumptions are psychically suspended, but these can powerfully affect bodily states. Bion's protomental matrix anticipates the work of Marty et al. (1963) and other writers of the French psychosomatic school, who have proposed that psychosomatic illness is a result of "foreclosed" emotional experience (McDougall, 1984; Schneider, 1995, 2003, 2007), which has been discharged into the body because it is too disturbing to elaborate psychically.

After publishing *Experiences in Groups* (1961), Bion rarely mentions the protomental matrix; however, it seems to be folded into his later ideas of alpha and beta elements in his theory of thinking, and eventually into his conceptualization of the self. In his last published paper (Bion, 1979), he discusses "the problem of communication within the self" (p. 324). In that paper, he alters the terms of the discussion: "I dislike terms that imply 'the body' and 'the mind,' therefore, I use 'self' to include what I call body and mind; and 'a mental space' for further ideas which may be developed" (pp. 324–325). Our primitive past, our present, and our future are interwoven in the self, which is made up of the entirety of our experiences.

Bion did not clearly distinguish protomental phenomena from beta elements when he moved from his theory of the protomental to his theory of alpha function (Bion, 1962). I expand on Bion's ideas here by suggesting that protomental phenomena are the unrepresentable but ever-present state of potentiality that exists as the origin of what may become thoughts. They are neither assimilated (alpha elements) nor unassimilated (beta elements) (Bion, 1992) but are the lowest level of sensory data registration and are automatic and reflexive. The underlying protomental state is latent until activated by contact with the outside world, which allows beta elements to form as the first primitive organization with the potential to be transformed into thoughts.

In a group, the basic assumptions are activated automatically from the protomental, with the potential either to be encoded as beta elements for evacuation, or transformed into alpha elements available for symbolic thinking in the work group. When the protomental elements do not undergo sufficient psychic realization to generate either of these processes, they continue as pre-beta phenomena in the form of a basic assumption. Therefore, they are not contained and cannot be used for dreaming or thinking (Ferro, 2002; Grotstein, 2000; Schneider, 2005c, 2010).

Bion was careful to keep the concept of protomental at the postulate level, and cautions the reader not to "establish a more rigid order of cause and effect than I wish to subscribe to, for clinically it is useful to consider these events as links in a circular series [of thoughts]" (1961, p. 101).

In his discussion of the protomental, Bion demonstrates how the mind works, and shows that we must be willing to be puzzled to allow the mind to think. He conveys the process through his tentative use of language that contains the seeds of his thinking. "I propose to postulate the existence of 'proto-mental' phenomena" (1961, p. 101). He continues, "It might prove useful . . . .. I cannot represent my view adequately without proposing a concept that transcends experience . . . if it throws light on what takes place." He emphasizes that "much can be lost by the exclusion of tentative theories that show how different ideas were developed" (1961, p. 7).

Bion's willingness to share unformed ideas demonstrates how he uses wild thoughts, and his meandering fragments convey something to the reader beyond the words that "might throw light on" developing his theory of the mind (1961, p. 101). "The meaning is revealed by the pattern formed and the light thus trapped – not by the structure, the carved work itself" (Bion, 1991, p. 190).

III – Experiencing in Groups

Fragments of Bion's Personal Experience with Groups

As analysts, we struggle with how to take in ideas from "the group" as we attempt to define ourselves to ourselves, and locate ourselves in relation to the analytic community without sacrificing our individuality. Early in his career, Bion moved among and beyond the influences of others to make something of his own, and also encouraged his peers to take what was original to him and make with it something of their own.

Bion served as president of the British Psychoanalytical Association, chair of the Melanie Klein Trust, and was a highly honored and frequently quoted psychoanalyst. Nevertheless, it seems that he did not feel "heard" in England, and he appeared to believe that his being revered was the problem: when people revere an individual, they do not listen to him. According to his wife, Francesca, Bion's refrain during his last years in London was: "[I'm] akin to being loaded with honors and sunk without a trace" (F. Bion, 1995, p. 15). His move to Los Angeles failed to solve the problem of not being heard:

> The relationship between myself and my colleagues here in Los Angeles could be accurately described as almost entirely unsuccessful. They are puzzled by and cannot understand me – but have some respect for what they cannot understand. There is, if I am not mistaken, more fear than understanding or sympathy for my

thoughts, personality, or ideas. There is no question of the situation – the emotional situation – being any better anywhere else. I could say much the same for England.

(Bion, 1992, p. 334)

Bion was acutely aware of the ubiquity of the dependency basic assumption mentality, which he found in all groups wherever he went. He seemed to feel tension not only between his original ideas and the ideas of those theorists who had influenced his thinking about groups – Trotter, Freud, and Klein – but also between himself and his peers in London and Los Angeles, who expected him to lead their groups. He seemed to resist becoming their thought leader, and strived – apparently without much success – to get them to think on their own, beyond his contributions, and may have been disappointed by those who made him into a sort of a mystic.

Although his *Experiences in Groups* (1961) had become popular much to his surprise (Bion, 1961, p. 7), Bion felt his thinking about groups and his theory of thinking in general had not greatly impacted psychoanalytic thought. In a letter to one of his children, Bion wrote: "The one book that I couldn't be bothered with, even when pressure was put on me 10 years later [*Experiences in Groups*], has been a continuous success" (F. Bion, 1985, p. 213). And earlier, in the introduction to *Experiences in Groups* (Bion, 1961), he admitted: "The articles printed here aroused more interest than I expected" (p. 7). It seems that Bion felt his original thinking about groups had been misunderstood by his professional colleagues, who appeared more interested in using his work as a therapeutic approach than elaborating a theory of thinking.

Basic Assumptions in the Analytic Dyad

Anyone who has employed a technique of investigation that depends on the presence of two people, and psychoanalysis is such a technique, can be regarded not only as taking part in the investigation of one mind by another, but also as investigating the mentality not of a group but of a pair.

(Bion, 1961, p. 62)

Bion refers to the dyad in analysis as a pair. For Bion, "the psycho-analytical situation is not 'individual psychology' but 'pair' [psychology]" (1961, p. 62). "Psychoanalysis, in the light of my experience of groups, can be regarded as a work group likely to stimulate the basic assumption of pairing" (p. 176).

Although Bion never specifically mentioned it, nor did he in any way develop the idea, it seems to me that in the course of individual analysis, breakdowns in the work group mentality stimulate the basic assumption pairing, with alpha function deteriorating into what may turn "the analysis itself into a piece of acting out" (1967, p. 87; see also Britton, 2013).

When the individual is in psychoanalysis or in-group analysis, thinking eventually triumphs over basic assumptions, dis-illusion over illusion, and reality over magical thinking. Bion writes, "The psychoanalytic problem is the problem of growth and its harmonious resolution in the relationships between the container and the contained, repeated in individual, pair, and finally, group (intra- and extra-psychically)" (1970, pp. 65–66). For the patient in a group, the group makes psychological what the individual is not yet able to give psychological form by turning the protomental into mental.

Bion leaves no doubt about the importance of the herd mentality in individual work. As individuals, we are always in semi-isolation, and coming into contact with the group or an individual analyst stimulates the basic situation and basic emotional drives, offering us the opportunity to transform the physical into the mental.

Group pressure is derived from a basic assumption group, fight-flight mentality in a patient's (or an analyst's) life – for instance, when an analysand feels persecuted or self-righteous toward the analyst as a consequence of what is occurring in the patient's group life at work. Group thinking affects psychoanalysis in another way as well. The pair is not a group, but the two are always part of larger groups within which they work. For example, when an analyst who is identified with a particular school of psychoanalysis works with a patient who is also an analyst and is identified with the same school, they share implicit viewpoints about the analysis, believing that their analytic approach is the best. They may share the basic assumptions of dependency upon a leader (whether it be Bion, Jung, Klein, Kohut, or anyone else), and the need to pair to create an analysis – a truth, "a Messiah" (1962, p. 152). They may experience the basic assumption of fight-flight relative to analysts identified with other analytic schools and their leaders.

As analysts and analysands, we bring these three conceptual categories – individual, pair, and group – to our thinking in the analytic situation. Our various group memberships have important consequences for our analytic work, as illustrated by Wallace (2007) in her communication of the personal and professional difficulties posed when her analysis was terminated after her training analyst was expelled from the institute as a consequence of ethical violations. Her communication can be seen as an example of her individual psychology and the relationship to past and present, her unconscious and conscious mind, and her struggle with the repressed unconscious.

As evidenced in Wallace's communication, the pair, individual transference, projective identification, the analytic third, analytic fields, and the mentality of the groups of which she and her analyst were members are all inextricably entwined. They constitute the field in which psychoanalysis is conducted, and demonstrate what can develop between the analyst and the patient – particularly when the analysis is part of training required by an institute, and the analyst has broken the laws of the pair and the group by acting out.

Part of what makes it exceptionally difficult to analyze a candidate within the structure of an institute training model is the pressure from the institute group. The analysis takes place and fulfills the requirement of the group, so both analyst and patient/candidate are agents of the institute; but the analyst is also the agent of the institute who must, at the very least, inform the institute whether or not the candidate has fulfilled the requirements of the institute. In this way, this analysis becomes a special category, because it is not being conducted exclusively for the psychological growth of the patient/candidate; it also serves the needs of the institute group.

Bion observed that:

> The apparent difference between group psychology and individual psychology is an illusion produced by the fact that the group provides an intelligible field of study for certain aspects of individual psychology, and in so doing brings into prominence phenomena that appear alien to an observer unaccustomed to using the group.
>
> (Bion, 1961, p. 34)

In other words, recognition of our "experiences in groups" is essential for the practice of psychoanalysis, whether that practice be with individuals or with groups. Group therapy training is not only therapeutic but also benefits the analyst's thinking. Bion says it gives analysts the experience of more easily recognizing and familiarizing themselves with the basic assumptions, which will then be more easily recognized when working in an analytic dyad.

To sum up, there are characteristics in the individual whose real significance cannot be understood unless it is recognized that they are part of his equipment as a herd animal. One cannot understand a recluse living in isolation unless one is informed about the group of which he is a member (Bion, 1961).

From this point of view, individual relationships originate from groups. Psychoanalysis requires that the analyst use binocular vision to be aware of when he and the patient are operating in basic assumption mentality or in work group mentality.

Summary and Conclusions

Bion's contributions to a psychoanalytic theory of groups foreshadow almost the entirety of his theoretical opus. I have discussed the influence of the work of Freud, Trotter, and Klein on Bion's thinking about groups, and the ways in which Bion radically and originally reshaped psychoanalytic thinking by using his experience with groups. He leaves us with a far-reaching but incomplete theory of a group instinct that is present in the individual in latent form at all times, and is therefore active in every analysis.

We usually do not think much about groups when we are with individual analysands. I suggest that to make only individual interpretations is to miss the tension between the patient and the analyst as members of the analytic dyad and of groups. By attending to the basic assumptions, we may become aware of the underlying latent – but ever-present – fight-flight, pairing, and dependency basic assumption mentalities. In each case, we see the interplay of the three basic assumptions – one prominent and the other two waiting in the wings.

A group mentality is of significance not in some of our analysands, but in all of them. Since it is innate and not related to past experience, it is a common denominator throughout our development during the course of a lifetime, and results in a constant struggle between what we might call our higher reasoning and our lower nature. What is revealed in an analysis that is otherwise hidden is the tension between the analysand's thinking and his innate, instinctual desire to be a member of a group.

Bion challenges us as readers to re-view what we believe we know and how we come to know it. He raises uncomfortable questions that destabilize our beliefs, leaving us with self-doubts that spur us to re-consider our understandings, and in so doing, he inspires us to think beyond Freud's, Trotter's, and Klein's ideas about groups – and even beyond his own.

Notes

1   No one has pointed out the inseparability of the life of the individual and the life of the group more forcefully or more beautifully than Joseph Conrad (1897/2008). "Few men realize that their life, the very essence of their character, their capabilities and their audacities . . . the courage, the composure, the confidence; the emotions and principles; every great and every significant thought belongs not to the individual but to the crowd: to the crowd that believes blindly in the irresistible force of its institutions and of its morals, in the power of its police and of its opinion" (p. 5).

2   My discussion of influence and originality in Bion's work has been informed by Ogden's (2006) discussion of Loewald, wherein he elaborates the concept of the "tension between influence and originality," and concludes that "no generation has the right to claim absolute originality for its creations," and yet "each new generation does contribute something uniquely of its own" (Ogden, 2006, p. 117). My intention is to extend the implications of Bion's work with groups to aspects of analytic thinking that lie beyond its relevance to group analysis.

3   As Ogden (2009) observed, "In that collection of papers (*Experiences in Groups*, 1961), Bion introduces a radical reformulation of the psychoanalytic conception of thinking and its psychopathology" (p. 92), which adumbrates almost all the major themes Bion developed in his subsequent writing.

4   "Man is altruistic because he must be, not because reason recommends it, for herd suggestion opposes any advance in altruism" (Trotter, 1916/2005, p. 46).

References

Bion, F. (Ed.) (1985). *All my sins remembered: Another part of a life and the other side of genius: Family letters.* Fleetwood Press.

Bion, F. (1995). The days of our years. *Journal of Melanie Klein Society & Object Relations, 13,* 1–30.

Bion, W. R. (1952). Group dynamics: A review. *International Journal of Psychoanalysis, 33,* 235–247.

Bion, W. R. (1959). Attacks on linking. *International Journal of Psychoanalysis, 40,* 308–314.

Bion, W. R. (1961). *Experiences in groups and other papers.* Basic Books.

Bion, W. R. (1962). *Learning from experience.* Basic Books.

Bion, W. R. (1963). *Elements of psychoanalysis.* Maresfield Library.

Bion, W. R. (1965). *Transformations.* Jason Aronson.

Bion, W. R. (1967). *Second thoughts.* Jason Aronson.

Bion, W. R. (1970). *Attention and interpretation: A scientific approach to insight in psychoanalysis and groups.* Tavistock.

Bion, W. R. (1978). *Four discussions with W. R. Bion.* Clunie Press.

Bion, W. R. (1979). Making the best of a bad job. *Bulletin of the British Psychoanalysis Society, 18,* 321–331.

Bion, W. R. (1990). *Brazilian lectures.* Karnac Books.

Bion, W. R. (1991). *A memoir of the future.* Karnac Books.

Bion, W. R. (1992). *Cogitations* (F. Bion, Ed). Karnac Books.

Bion, W. R. (2005). *The Tavistock seminars* (F. Bion, Ed.). Karnac Books.

Britton, R. B. (2010). Personal communication.

Britton, R. B. (2013). Commentary on three papers by Wilfred R. Bion. *Psychoanalytic Quarterly, 82,* 311–321.

Conrad, J. (2008). An outpost of progress. In *Tales of unrest.* Echo Library. (Original work published 1897)

Ferro, A. (2002). Some implications of Bion's thought. *International Journal of Psychoanalysis, 83,* 597–607.

Freud, S. (1961a). Beyond the pleasure principle, group psychology, and other works. In J. Strachey (Ed. & Trans.), *The standard edition of the complete psychological works of Sigmund Freud* (Vol. 18, pp. 67–134). Hogarth Press. (Original work published 1922)

Freud, S. (1961b). Group psychology and the analysis of the ego. In J. Strachey (Ed. & Trans.), *The standard edition of the complete psychological works of Sigmund Freud* (Vol. 18, pp. 67–134). Hogarth Press. (Original work published 1921)

Freud, S. (1961c). The ego and the id. In J. Strachey (Ed. & Trans.), *The standard edition of the complete psychological works of Sigmund Freud* (Vol. 19, pp. 3–66). Hogarth Press. (Original work published 1923)

Freud, S. (1962). Civilization and its discontents. In J. Strachey (Ed. & Trans.), *The standard edition of the complete psychological works of Sigmund Freud* (Vol. 21, pp. 59–145). Hogarth Press. (Original work published 1930 [1929])

Grotstein, J. S. (2000). *Who is the dreamer who dreams the dream? A study of psychic presences.* Analytic Press.

Jones, E. (1940). Wilfred Trotter. *International Journal of Psychoanalysis, 2,* 114.

Klein, M. (1952). Notes on some schizoid mechanisms. In M. Klein, S. Isaacs, P. Heimann, & J. Riviere, Eds.), *Developments in psychoanalysis.* Hogarth Press. (Original work published 1946)

Lacan, J. (1966). *Écrits.* Seuil.

Loewald, H. (1980). The waning of the Oedipus complex. In *Papers on psychoanalysis* (pp. 384–404). Yale University Press.

Maddox, B. (2006). *Freud's Wizard: Ernest Jones and the transformation of psychoanalysis.* John Murray.

Marty, P., de M'Uzan, M., & David, C. (1963). *L' Investigation psychosomatique.* Presses Universitaires de France.

McDougall, J. (1984). The "disaffected" patient: reflections on affect pathology. *Psychoanalytic Quarterly, 53,* 384–409.

Ogden, B. H., & Ogden, T. H. (2013). *The analyst's ear and the critic's eye: Rethinking psychoanalysis and literature.* Routledge.

Ogden, T. H. (2006). Reading Loewald: Oedipus reconceived. In *Rediscovering psychoanalysis: Thinking, dreaming, learning, and forgetting.* Routledge.

Ogden, T. H. (2009). Bion's four principles of mental functioning. In *Rediscovering psychoanalysis: Thinking, dreaming, learning, and forgetting.* Routledge.

Ogden, T. H. (2011). Personal communication.

Schneider, J. A. (1995). Eating disorders, addictions, and unconscious fantasy. *Bulletin of the Menninger Clinic, 59,* 177–190.

Schneider, J. A. (2003). Janus-faced resilience in the analysis of a severely traumatized patient. *Psychoanalytic Review, 90,* 869–887.

Schneider, J. A. (2005a). Experiences in K and – K. *International Journal of Psychoanalysis, 86,* 825–839.

Schneider, J. A. (2005b). Reply to Dr. Alexander. *International Journal of Psychoanalysis, 86,* 1479.

Schneider, J. A. (2005c). Dreaming the truth of experience: Heaven. *Psychoanalytic Review, 92,* 777–785.

Schneider, J. A. (2007). Panic as a form of foreclosed experience. *Psychoanalytic Quarterly, 76,* 1293–1316.

Schneider, J. A. (2009). Signs and symbols in Dersu Uzsala. *Psychoanalytic Review, 96,* 173–180.

Schneider, J. A. (2010). From Freud's dream-work to Bion's work of dreaming: The changing conception of dreaming in psychoanalytic theory. *International Journal of Psychoanalysis, 91,* 521–540

Trotter, W. R. (1916). *Instincts of the herd in peace and war.* Unwin.

Trotter, W. R. (1941). *The collected papers of Wilfred Trotter.* Oxford University. Press.

Trotter, W. R. (2005). *Instincts of the herd in peace and war.* Cosimo. (Original work published 1916)

Wallace, E. M. (2007). Losing a training analyst for ethical violations: A candidate's perspective. *International Journal of Psychoanalysis, 88,* 1275–1288.

4

Panic as a Form of Foreclosed Experience

I have found that, very often, the psychic processes underlying the symptoms of patients who experience states of panic[1] seem very similar to those I encounter in my psychoanalytic work with patients experiencing psychosomatic disorders. Patients experiencing certain types of panic disorders and patients with psychosomatic disorders appear limited in their ability to use verbal interpretations effectively for conscious and unconscious psychological work. In any analysis, words themselves convey only a part of what the analyst communicates to the patient, while other parts of the communication are conveyed by tone of voice, facial expression and other bodily movements, lapses of memory, actings-in, and so on. But in analytic work with certain types of patients manifesting panic states, words seem to have particularly little communicative value.

Under such circumstances, I find myself relying on nonverbal dimensions of communication far more heavily than in my work with neurotic patients, and even in that with some psychotic patients. I have further found it useful to view this asymbolic symptomatology as a form of foreclosure: an almost total removal from the psyche (McDougall, 1989) and relegation to the body of undreamable experience (Bion, 1962/1977) that has its origin in infantile and childhood traumatic emotional experience. The infant, and later the child, due to maternal failure to hold and contain primitive experience (Grotstein, 2000; Ogden, 2004a), is left to manage on his or her own.

Most often, panic is thought of as severe anxiety associated with phobic states or with psychotic disintegration. Less frequently has it been conceived as a form of foreclosure involving a virtually total repudiation of symbolization that bypasses psychic regulation and settles for a discharge of excitation directly into the body as somatic illness. In this chapter, I propose that, in some patients, states of panic involve a form of foreclosure[2] similar to that of dis-affected patients (McDougall, 1984, 1989), alexithymic patients (Nemiah & Sifneos, 1970), and those with severe perversions (de M'Uzan, 2003).

Although de M'Uzan suggests that "the perverse solution . . . lends itself particularly well to observation [of foreclosure]," he goes on to broaden the terms of this argument:

> But other outcomes are conceivable, such as . . . [the] almost mute development of a severe somatic pathology . . . as if the "somatoses" were the equivalent of an act,

DOI:10.4324/9781003384601-4

admittedly involuntary, . . . where it triggers somatic, not hysterical symptoms . . . "acting in."

(2003, pp. 717–718)

De M'Uzan is referring here to an "acting in" the body – a non-human-related, non-symbolic evacuation of excitation into the body as somatic illness, which the organism abides as if the body had a mind of its own. De M'Uzan's psychic foreclosure involves thinking that is operational, i.e., removed from the internal psychic world, non-affective and non-personal.

All of these disorders (psychosomatic illness, dis-affected states, alexithymia, and panic states) share a defining characteristic: there is a failure of symbolization and a relegation to the body of what, under other psychological circumstances, may have become thoughts and feelings. Analysis of these disorders is incompatible with the classic theoretical approach: "*psychoanalytic processes are the antithesis of psychosomatic processes* . . . they demand a different approach from that required to understand the neurotic parts of the personality" (McDougall, 1974, p. 439) "in psychosomatic illness, the body does its own 'thinking'" (p. 441).

In the clinical discussion that follows, I describe the movement of a patient who was initially unable to make a connection between his panic state and events in his inner or outer life, or to link ideas in the analysis. From his wordless, asymbolic, unspeakable experience in the body, the patient progressed to the point that he was able to begin to generate a psychological state of mind (more accurately, a state of the psyche-soma) in which he managed to express feelings and create personal meaning from his experience, albeit in quite jumbled, disorganized speech. At a critical point in the analysis, the patient began to make use of his body in a symbolic way in the office waiting room, and, eventually, was able to communicate using verbally symbolic language (including metaphor). The presentation of this clinical work illustrates my conception of panic as a form of foreclosure, as well as an approach to working with such states analytically.

I

Working With and Without Words

As I opened the door to meet Mr. A for our initial consultation session, he was sitting in a chair in the corner of the waiting room, moving his palm and fingertips along the wall. Though I felt that I had intruded upon him, he gave no indication of being startled. I had the feeling that he was using my waiting room as his private sanctuary.

Once seated in my consulting room, Mr. A carefully surveyed the room in silence. He then commented on the analytic couch, the books on the shelf, and my necktie. After a brief pause, Mr. A said in a matter-of-fact way, "An unpleasant incident occurred today. I'm trying to figure out what happened. It occurred at 9:30 this morning when I was in my boss's office for my annual performance review. My stomach was bothering me. I felt my chest tighten. What if I couldn't read the words on the review my boss was about to hand me? I ran into the bathroom. It was hard to take in air, hard to breathe. My heart was pounding. I felt it getting bigger. The room was spinning, thoughts were racing through my mind – I thought I was dying. I told myself, 'Indigestion – you know you have digestion problems.' I couldn't go back to the meeting, so I just left."

Mr. A seemed oblivious to any emotional connection between his anxiety state and the meeting with his boss or his initial meeting with me. Neither did he seem to notice that he was talking to me as if we had been working together in analysis for a long time. With all this in mind, I said to him, "It seems that your meeting with your boss and your meeting with me have stirred things up inside of you and let loose a physical reaction that so took you by surprise that you were at a loss to know what to make of it."

Mr. A quickly and pleasantly contradicted me by saying, "Oh, no, my take on the meeting with the boss was that my reaction was just a good old, garden-variety upset stomach – nothing more, nothing less. What I'm trying to figure out is why I wasn't able to say no to eating that brownie."

I was surprised by Mr. A's rejection of my idea that his annual review and his initial meeting with me may have been more frightening to him than he realized, and that his bodily sensations might have something to do with his emotional state. When I tried for a second time to link the patient's physical/emotional response to the meetings with his boss and me, he responded by saying, "I wish I could say that these meetings made today a difficult day, but today was no different from any other day."

After this second dismissal of the seemingly self-evident connections I was suggesting, I felt confused, and wondered if he was acting obtuse in a passive-aggressive way. A patient's dismissal of what I have to say is not uncommon – but what struck me about Mr. A was his almost-complete inability or unwillingness to entertain the possibility of a link between his physical state and emotional meaning.

In our next session, Mr. A repeated his description of the meeting with his boss, giving virtually the same details, neither elaborating nor condensing. While I said nothing in response, I was aware that my attempts to attribute psychological meaning to Mr. A's experience had not been utilizable by him. I wondered if he was able to think or dream about (i.e., to do unconscious psychological work with) any of his lived emotional experience.

As he was talking, I had a fleeting memory of consoling my distraught son while driving him to preschool some years earlier – a reverie that later proved valuable in my work with Mr. A.

II

After several more sessions, we began meeting four times a week, and Mr. A began using the couch.[3] He was a tall, thin, rather soft-spoken man in his mid-40s, the first of two children of "hardworking parents." He told me his father managed an automobile dealership and was often away from home while traveling to neighboring states to purchase cars. When at home, his father was irritable and hit the patient "to discipline me." Mr. A described his mother as "depressed for as long as I can remember." He said that she was someone who "cooked the meals, did the shopping, changed the beds, and cleaned the toilets." As he told me about his parents, he showed no emotion, speaking in a flat, monotonic voice, as if relating someone else's childhood history, a history completely foreign to himself.

Mr. A was born prematurely and spent his first 3 months in an incubator under bright heat lamps as a treatment for jaundice caused by blood incompatibility. Due to medical complications, his mother also remained in the hospital for the first 5 months after his birth, and continued afterward to suffer from poor health. During his childhood, he was required to play outside with his friends so as not to disturb his mother's rest.

When school let out for the summer, Mr. A and his younger sister were immediately sent to their aunt's and uncle's home in the country. The patient slept by himself in a small trailer on the corner of the property because there was not enough room in the house. Mr. A told me that he had always been petrified about staying in the trailer. He worried that someone would break into the trailer (he had seen a TV show in which the chest of a man opened up and let out a strange alien creature). He never slept well, but as summer approached, his sleep became far more disturbed. When he told his mother how terrified he was, she said, "Oh, what are you afraid of – Auntie and Uncle are right next door." As Mr. A told me about his childhood terror, again, I was struck by the unemotional manner in which he spoke, with no shift in the tone of his voice or in his facial expression.

At this point, I suspected Mr. A's anxiety was a reflection of his only partially successful effort to ward off forbidden, dangerous thoughts and feelings – namely, that his parents had not been parents to him. But I still felt at sea. Often during these early sessions, I found myself fighting to stay awake as Mr. A talked. At other times, I felt anxious and experienced a sense of futility about ever being able to understand what was going on in the analysis. My reveries while with him were sparse and of little help to me.

During the first 2 years of the analysis, Mr. A often demanded that I tell him the meaning of something by saying, for example, "You surely must know." He would desperately ask me to tell him that "everything was going to be all right" and begged me to "say those words." He believed that I had "the answer," and that I was stubbornly and cruelly refusing to give him "the magic envelope with the answer in it." He was seemingly pleading for more of my words – spoken or written – but as our work seemed at a standstill, I was increasingly convinced that my words were of little use to him.

III

As Mr. A's analysis went on, I came to feel that any effort on my part to attribute meaning to what was happening between us (or in any other sector of his life) was futile. The sessions seemed to last for hours. I very frequently wondered whether the analysis was an analysis in form only. Mr. A seemed to believe that there was no meaning to his anxiety – it just was. It was like the furniture to which he referred at the start of each meeting, apparently in an effort to reacquaint himself with inanimate objects with which he felt familiar.

On several occasions after I had informed Mr. A that I had to cancel an upcoming meeting, he *later* stood at the entry to my office building and took a mental snapshot – a "picture postcard," as he described it. Once, when he returned from a holiday trip to a city on the East Coast, he told me that he had visited the city's psychoanalytic institute, where he roamed the halls looking admiringly at the photos on the wall. He told me this in a way that might be used to describe a pilgrimage to an art museum or a religious shrine.

I was confused by his seemingly not having any interest, much less awareness, of the meaning or significance of what he told me. He seemed indifferent and unable to differentiate between facts and emotions. I wondered if his lack of affect was the most significant aspect of the communication, that is, his showing me the juxtaposition of his registering my absence while not being able to experience or talk about his emotional response to it.

Only much later did I realize that Mr. A's experience was all "emotionally equivalent" – any one thing was as good or bad as anything else. I was reminded of Ogden's (1982) work on a state of "non-experience" in which "all things, people, places and behaviors are emotionally interchangeable. People, places, and objects are perceived, registered, and physically differentiated" (p. 147). I also reread McDougall's (1984, 1989) descriptions of dis-affected states.

Several months later, Mr. A began a session by saying rather compliantly, "I suppose I should tell you a dream. In the dream, it was morning and I woke up, went to the bathroom, and got ready to come to our session. Then I was here in this office during our regular daytime session – and you were you – and the setting was the same." He went on to say, "I started to collect the data about the dream. Funny, isn't it – the walls and everything else in the room were white. Like a blank screen, so there's not much more to say." I thought that his blank-screen imagery depicted the absence – both in our sessions and in his life – of personal meaning in his thoughts, feelings, and bodily sensations.

As Mr. A spoke, I thought briefly of another patient, Ms. C, who came to me for help with involuntary blinking (blepharospasm). She was extremely sensitive to light and, over the course of years, experienced increasing difficulty keeping her eyes open. Even while watching television, she preferred to keep her eyes nearly closed so that she would not blink involuntarily. For over 40 years, Ms. C had been a partner in a "good" marriage. In our first session, after telling me about the blinking symptom, she said that she was devoted to her husband and felt in love with him. But several months earlier, her husband had begun drinking excessively and having an affair with his secretary. After she gave me a litany of medical causes for her problem, I asked Ms. C what her response was to having discovered that her husband was having an affair. What struck me about her reply was the lifeless monotone of her voice as she told me that everything was "fine," and then blurted out, "I have no reason to feel malice or resentment toward my husband – why would I?" And for emphasis, she restated, "I want it understood – no malice toward him."

Both Ms. C and Mr. A denied the link between their physical symptoms and their emotional experience – a link that I, perhaps overzealously, had tried to demonstrate to Mr. A ("to sell him on" – as Mr. A's salesman father would have put it). With the feelings and images from my reverie of Ms. C in mind, my doubts increased about my earlier hypothesis concerning the underlying nature of Mr. A's anxiety. His inability to respond to my verbal interventions and his capacity to take in only a small part of what I was offering suggested to me that his "denied fearfulness" was not a neurotic anxiety founded on dangerous repressed thoughts and feelings. Rather, it began to occur to me that his "fear" had not become a feeling with meaningful linkages to other thoughts, feelings, memories, bodily sensations, and so on, but instead was experienced almost entirely in bodily form.

I said to Mr. A, "In telling me how your dream became a blank screen, I think you're trying to tell me how bleak the analysis feels to you and how blank I am to you. There are no landmarks, no punctuation, nothing surprising, interesting, or frightening."

Mr. A then said, "To have a thought about you, I have to work on it. Suppose I have a thought and it's wrong. The cost of working it out is high. This is like a tea dance. The answer is, there is no answer; there is no thought. So I have to be right. I have to understand. As frightened as I am, I can see the books on your shelf, and the books are good – words are inside of them and words will make it all okay. At least when I leave here today, I'll know I've done this – I've talked."

I viewed this sudden shift in Mr. A's focus onto my books as a retreat both from my having used words to communicate – which was in itself felt to be dangerous – and from my more accurate use of words. He quickly focused on the books as containers not of ideas expressed by a living person in words, but as sequences of words spoken by no one, which never changed. But I also felt that the patient's speech, in which one sentence was only very loosely tied to the next, was nonetheless an attempt to use words to say something that held meaning for him. Perhaps at this point in the analysis, books were not simply interchangeable things but sanctuaries in which words, meanings, coherence of feeling could be hidden and preserved. It seemed that Mr. A was caught between two equally terrible choices: on the one hand, risking the disintegration of his mind if he were to attempt to think his thoughts and feel his feelings; and, on the other, living in a world virtually devoid of thought, feeling, or personal meaning.

I said to Mr. A, "I think that when our roles feel rote and fully expected, it helps you feel safe with me." Mr. A did not respond, remaining silent for a very long time. Then he said, "Nothing to say – unless I have some traumatic experience to justify it. I think the best session was when I came in here in the throes of my heart racing. I was all over the place." Mr. A continued, "I should just leave." He said that he could not come up with any more thoughts. (It was very close to the end of the session.) He then got off the couch and walked out of the office.

As I sat alone, I thought that, having begun to open himself up to words, ideas, and feelings – both his own and mine – Mr. A became afraid of hearing the meaning carried by my words, including the words "time is up." Instead of allowing an emotional event to occur – such as the end of the meeting – he preempted the opportunity to experience a feeling by leaving. Perhaps he was also beginning to "make a statement" with his actions. In this instance, the statement may have involved the feeling and idea that his physical absence was more real than anything he could say about absence, and that it was important for him to feel in control of that absence in any way he could.

Less than an hour after this session in which Mr. A abruptly departed, I had an episode of rapid, irregular heartbeat (I was not aware of experiencing fear). I had first experienced an arrhythmia of this sort on a recent trek in Nepal at very high altitudes; I was afraid that the current episode of arrhythmia meant that I had permanently affected my heart in Nepal and that I was having a heart attack. This fear was so pressing that I decided a few hours after the session to get an EKG. Only when the results showed that my heart was functioning normally did I wonder if my reaction was a primitive identification – an instance of my temporarily experiencing Mr. A's unfelt fear.

IV

I had noticed from the beginning of our work together that Mr. A would often use a string of words to start our meetings. On many occasions, after commenting on a new magazine in the waiting room, a notepad on my desk, or the quality of light in the room, he would say, "Okay, okay, okay, come on, come on. I don't know where to start today – I don't know what to do." I had come to understand that in so saying, Mr. A was grasping for thoughts and ideas.

I said to him on one of these occasions, "From the sound of your voice, there is no mistaking that things are anything but okay. If things were okay, and you were able to have thoughts and feelings that you were able to connect with one another, you wouldn't feel so empty and feel that there is no option other than to have me think and speak for you. That leaves you in a state of terrible paralysis."

Mr. A responded by saying, "On Monday [which was the first session after we had agreed to meet at a new time] when I left here, I was really frightened. It seemed like the plant behind my head had claws. You're part of what's frightening. What happened was I wasn't able to shut you out. It's like walking off the edge of a cliff and falling forever. Or looking out the window and not being able to close the blinds." He went on to say, "I couldn't speak. It was as though I was in this room and all the oxygen was taken out. I could open my mouth, but I couldn't speak."

I told Mr. A that, for the first time, he seemed able to hold onto a feeling that had upset him during the previous session, and then to bring it in to talk with me about it. (I thought, but did not say, that my not being with him between sessions had led him to feel that he would never be able to live and think on his own, and that he was doomed to live forever with the "blinds closed" to his feelings.) Mr. A was attempting a new openness with me. As he expressed it: "When I see you, I make progress; when I don't see you, I don't step in the right direction. That sounds really confused, like analysis is a touchstone for my self. When I smell the perfume and feel the warmth of your previous patient on the couch, I know you have lots to say to them and they back to you."

The most significant development of this period of analysis was the emergence of the patient's (nascent) capacity to connect different parts of his emotional experience.

In this instance, he linked his separations from me with his feelings of bodily terror ("falling forever"). Similarly, he was able to connect his being with me with his feelings of sensorial groundedness and (in fantasy which was experienced as fact) his being able to have a genuine conversation with me ("I know you have lots to say to them and they back to you").

It seemed to me that Mr. A was beginning to speak to me in a way that suggested he was in a transitional state in which he was moving in and out of verbally symbolic thinking and communicating. At one point, he described his tension by saying, "The tension builds up to the point of feeling like I'm being charged up with energy – like having D batteries in my fingers." His use of metaphor represented a significant advance from a virtually asymbolic state to one in which he was beginning to genuinely feel his emotions: "I can talk here, so I can experience something."

At this point in our work, something occurred that clarified for me the nature of Mr. A's experience and alerted me to the critical role of our nonverbal communication. One day, as I approached the waiting room to meet Mr. A, I expected the room to be empty because I could not see a human figure through the frosted glass panel in the center of the door. To my surprise, as I opened the door, I found him stretched out on his back on the floor in a way that filled the space. His eyes were bulging slightly, and his eyelids were slowly opening and closing.

I stopped in my tracks and said hesitatingly, "Mr. A?" in a tone of voice that suggested I was not sure whom I was addressing. I felt alarmed. Was I witnessing a petit mal seizure or a heart attack? (I later wondered if he were taking back into himself the heart attack – tachycardia, or an "attack" on my heart – that I had earlier experienced "for him.") He lay still, making no move to get up. As I towered over him, I felt removed, so I pulled up a chair and sat close to him. I sensed his fear and began talking calmly to him. I found myself describing what I imagined it felt like to lie on the floor. I said, "The feel of the floor on your back must feel solid to you."

As I sat there with Mr. A, I was again reminded of an incident that had occurred while I was driving my son to preschool (which, in a sense, had also included an "attack on the heart"). My son was sitting silently in the back seat of the car, looking self-absorbed and dejected. When I asked him how things were going at school, I could see in the rearview mirror a look of sadness on his face as he said, "Good." He said nothing more as tears welled up in his eyes and began rolling down his cheeks. I asked a number of questions in an attempt to determine what was wrong. Was he upset about something that had happened at school or at home, with me or with his friends? As we neared his school, I could see that he was becoming increasingly frightened but trying to keep his feelings in check. Then I did something I had never done before: I pulled the car over to the side of the road, got out, and sat in the back seat next to him. I just sat quietly with him – not waiting for a response, but just being with him.

As my thoughts returned to Mr. A lying on the floor in front of me, it became all the more clear to me that my physical presence and the sound of my voice were more important than the content of what I was saying. We continued in this way for several minutes – I talked slowly, pausing often to think. He told me that he had felt overwhelmed and full of anxiety and did not know what to do. He had stretched himself out on the floor to feel something firm against his back as he sometimes did at home. After a while, he settled down and was able to get up. As I followed him into the office, a word came to mind, which I thought but did not say – grounded. Mr. A was trying to achieve groundedness, and I had achieved groundedness from getting to know him over the time we had worked together. So even though this was a surprising event, it did not lead me to feel anxious. I had felt useful to Mr. A in the waiting room – which was a very rare event in this analysis.

Mr. A was then silent for several minutes. I suspected that he had no words or even feelings, but only sensations of something unknown, frightening, and without definition. After a time, I broke the silence by saying, "I may be wrong, but I think that you didn't have even a trace of a thought, or even of a feeling, to bring into the office with you today. In a sense, you were disconnected from yourself and had nothing with which to connect yourself with me."

He responded, "What you say makes sense, but you and the office did not even exist. I was in the middle of a strange experience. I'm still feeling disconnected and anxious. I was rushing to your office. By the time I got here, I was so tightly wound, I was out of my head."

Mr. A was telling me about a profound sense of alienation from himself and from everything and everyone else. His use of the phrase "out of my head" suggested that his bodily reaction had taken over his mental state. He was out of his mind and existing almost completely in a world of bodily sensations, in a body that did not even feel like his own. He was showing me in the waiting room that his panic was a bodily explosion that substituted for a thought, dream, feeling, or fantasy. But to leave it at that would be to miss the way in which Mr. A was no longer simply experiencing these things; he was beginning to show them to me and to tell me about them. In other words, we had the beginnings of two people talking to one another. My reacting calmly to the waiting room event seemed to have been instrumental in helping Mr. A show me and tell me his difficulties in a more symbolically mediated way – first by the use of his body and later in words.

Mr. A began the next session by telling me what had become a familiar dream about getting up and coming to my office, but this time, he added, "There was a difference in your office colors – purple and lavender. The wall colors were very clear in the dream; in the past, the walls were a chalky white. You handed me some notes – very specific things – very clear, as if saying, 'Here are the notes.' And I took them from you and put them on the table. I didn't need them. I started saying something." He was again silent for several minutes, during which a subtle shift in feeling tone occurred.

In contrast to previous dreams, which were "black and white," in this dream, Mr. A colored the walls purple and lavender. It seemed to me that he both wanted me to think and speak for him (to give him my notes) and at the same time felt that he no longer needed that from me (he put the notes on the table). I said to Mr. A, "In this dream, the office has more color; you have your own thoughts, and you don't need mine as substitutes for yours." He was silent for a very long time, and then responded, "Yes, that feels true – I can't say any more than what I've already said today."

Midway into the 5th year of analysis, after starting an hour with a brief period of silence, Mr. A said: "Funny, but this thought just popped into my head. Every June, my uncle bought a wild stallion at government auction and hired a guy named C. J. to train it. C. J. set up a round corral to work in. With a rectangular corral, the horse will run into a corner and stop because it has to. In a circular corral, it will run longer and stop because it wants to rather than being cornered and kicking. I hadn't thought of it like this before, but C. J. taught me the difference between breaking a horse and training it. With training, a gradual teamwork forms – a shared knowledge of one another. The horse will come to you. And when roping cows, it will stop before you rein it in. A broken horse needs to be steered, it is in constant fear, and will only respond when you are on its back, telling it what to do."

He became silent, and I said nothing, but I recognized that he had just told me a genuine thought that had "popped into" his head, a thought about what it felt like being with me at that moment. Not only was this a genuine thought in the moment; it also gathered into itself the history of the transference. In the beginning of my work with Mr. A, it was as if I were chasing him around and trying to corral him, but as my way of working with him changed over time, Mr. A's response to me also changed.

Discussion

My initial response to Mr. A's report of his anxiety attack was to attempt to understand his words as if they were symbolic representations of his thoughts, feelings, bodily states, and so on. I made (projected) links between his symptomatology and the unconscious content I attributed to it – for example, by viewing his anxiety during his meetings with his boss as a reflection of unconscious conflict. Rather than staying with his wordless (sensation-based) experience and living with the anxiety of not knowing (Schneider, 2005a), of proceeding while feeling completely in the dark, I was giving my own verbally symbolic form to his asymbolic fear. It was as if I were saying, "There's nothing to be afraid of [echoing his mother's response to his childhood fear of staying in his uncle's trailer] – I can give you words for the wishes and fears from which you are fleeing."

In retrospect, I realized that when I met Mr. A for our first session, his initial communication to me was a nonverbal, sensation-based experience of moving his hand along the waiting room wall, feeling the realness of its texture, which in turn lent a sense of realness to him through a "second skin formation"[4] (Bick, 1968, 1986; Tustin, 1981, 1990). In the consulting room, Mr. A continued his focus on objects in the room, which he connected like a child's dot-to-dot puzzle, forming a physical safety net within which to attempt to maintain the sense of a perimeter. He then told me about what had happened to him earlier that day – "The room was spinning, thoughts were racing through my mind – I thought I was dying." He was not telling me about having become frightened by the emotional situation; he was telling me about a sensation storm that had occurred suddenly, unexpectedly.

When he returned the following day and recounted almost verbatim the same story, I realized that he had not processed the panic state or the experience of meeting with me, and that he was unable to dream his experience, to use Bion's (1962/1977) expression. He was showing me (without conscious or unconscious intention) that he was not able to experience the most elementary events that made up his life – what Bion calls beta elements, which begin as protomental sense impressions associated with emotional experience. Because the protomental system is one "in which physical and psychological or mental are undifferentiated . . . it stands to reason that, when distress from this source manifests itself, it can manifest itself just as well in physical forms as in psychological" (Bion, 1959, p. 102).[5] These "raw sense impressions – related to an emotional experience" (Bion, 1962/1977, p. 17), or beta elements, must become symbolic (converted into alpha elements) through a process of mentalization termed alpha function. In the absence of alpha function, two alternatives exist for dealing with unmediated psychic experience: expulsion either into space or into the body.

At the start of the analysis, I was attempting to make sense of Mr. A's anxiety symptoms in terms of the emergence of repressed conflicts. The failure of my early interpretations led to a long period of seemingly unproductive analysis. Only over time was I able to reframe for myself what was going on. I was then able to talk to Mr. A in a way consistent with the view that his symptoms reflected a severe compromise of both his symbolizing function and his capacity for conscious and unconscious psychological work. My own formulations became less focused on unconscious conflict and regression, and more concerned with Mr. A's difficulty in attributing meaning to his experience.

Only when I was able to sit beside Mr. A as he lay on the floor of the waiting room did I fully understand how premature my previous verbal interpretations had been. It was only after the situation began to change, during and following the waiting room incident, that I became aware of the degree to which he had relied on encapsulating reactions[6] (Tustin, 1986, 1990) and on the use of autistic objects[7] – a narrowing down of focus. Both these forms of defense had served – and, to a large extent, were continuing to serve – to limit his stimulation at the bodily level (which he was helpless to convert into thinking).

I hypothesized that Mr. A converted potential thoughts and feelings into sensation-based shapes and forms in the immediate environment (for example, the feel of the texture of the wall in the waiting room as he ran his hand along it). In this way, he created a place of safety at the skin surface, a "second skin formation" (Bick, 1968, 1986), attempting to maintain the continuity and integrity of his skin surface. This helped him fend off the sensation/feeling of panic, which for him took the form of a feeling of falling into endless space. Mr. A's use of an encapsulating form of defense may have been influenced by separation from his mother for an extended period of time shortly after birth – a separation that must have constituted a severe failure of maternal containment.

I was straddling the sensory and the verbal in a number of ways, which is best exemplified in the session that began with the patient lying on the waiting room floor. The sound of what I was saying was as important as the meaning of my words. Moreover, in both my thinking and speaking, I used words that were sensory in meaning. For example, I said to Mr. A that "the floor must feel solid," and in my mind, I used the word *grounded* to describe both the feeling of Mr. A's back against the solid floor and his being centered in himself. The different meanings of the word reflected my awareness of the patient's movement from one form of registering his psychic experience to another – from the concrete/sensory to the abstract.

Mr. A's thinking was "operational," an extension of action (de M'Uzan, 2003), and even though it appeared that we were talking, the exchange was two-dimensional, devoid of affect or self-reflection on the patient's part, and, to a considerable degree, lacking reflection on my part as well.

There was an autistic quality to the way he thought and the way he related to shapes and textures – potential thoughts and feelings were foreclosed from psychic elaboration and from connection with other thoughts and feelings in the process of thinking and dreaming his experience. The ultimate foreclosure is autism. Over time, I came to understand this state in terms of what Bion (1962/1977) referred to as a beta screen[8] (a pseudocommunication – or, perhaps more accurately, an anticommunication). As I now conceive of it, his racing thoughts were not thoughts that could be linked in the process of dreaming or thinking, but an epiphenomenon of an adrenergic, autonomic nervous system response – a direct bodily response to danger. His fear that his heart was beating so fast that he would die strongly suggests he was generating experience primarily in a sensation-dominated way (what Ogden refers to as an "autistic-contiguous mode of generating experience" [1989, p. 51]). The objects in my office environment (furniture, books, etc.) provided Mr. A with a way to organize himself by means of their complete predictability.

The analysis underwent a significant change once I was able to make psychological use of my reverie concerning the event while driving my son to preschool, a reverie in which I had no words to express my feelings. This helped me to symbolically represent for myself my experience of sitting quietly with Mr. A as he lay stretched out on my waiting room floor. I simply sat with Mr. A, thinking and talking quietly – not waiting for a response, but being with him and witnessing the experience that he was unable to put into words. I was able to hear what was not spoken, and I responded to him calmly and patiently in a way that was informed by my reverie. I was transforming the situation analytically (and yet not using verbal interpretations).[9]

As I became more receptive to direct, unmediated communications from Mr. A, I was better able to contain the patient's raw projections and to hold them without blocking or projecting them back into him too quickly and without adequate containing/dreaming.[10] Eventually, I was able to register and do psychological work with (something like) his experience.

My reverie concerning Ms. C, a former patient with a psychosomatic disorder, led me to think of the confusion I had experienced in treating her, and the way that she foreclosed her experience from psychic elaboration. I began to understand Mr. A's symptomatology, including his panic states, as foreclosed thoughts and feelings that were experienced somatically. His descriptions of his experience sounded as if he were talking about feelings such as anxiety, fear, terror, or panic. But, as I gradually learned, he was speaking of disturbing physical sensations that I associated with the experience of fear or panic, whose ancestor in nosological terms was Freud's actual neurosis occurring right now – with no connection to the past and no regulation of the present through mentalization. In Bion's language, "he [the patient] cannot be unaware of any single sensory stimulus: yet such hypersensitivity is not contact with reality" (Bion, 1962/1977, p. 8).[11]

Mr. A was suffering from a psychosomatic disorder (soma split off from psyche) no less than Ms. C had been. In psychosomatic disorders, the patient presents pathology of the psyche-soma in the form of a dysfunction of the body. In the case of Mr. A, there was a storm of adrenergic, autonomic nervous system activity – his body went nuts instead of his mind going nuts. Mr. A's body became the repository of the strain of unthinkable thoughts and feelings that could not be felt – a realm of racing thoughts, racing heart, hyperventilation, vertigo, and so on. Furthermore, my episode of irregular heartbeat seems to have represented my own experience of a feeling of fear that Mr. A had been unable to experience as a feeling.

As Mr. A began to be able to give symbolic form to his thoughts, feelings, and bodily sensations, he was at times difficult for me to follow. His sporadic incoherence in later sessions did not appear to be a return to operational and asymbolic experiences; rather, it seemed to me that his thinking reflected his beginning to be able to generate thoughts and keep them in mind (as opposed to in body), albeit in fragmented, disjointed form. I came to regard him as caught between two terrifying choices: psychotic breakdown if he were to allow potentially overwhelming feelings to be felt; or feeling nothing at all by foreclosing lived experience before it could be psychically elaborated. As he moved out of a foreclosed state of non-experience, his first experience (which had been previously avoided) was a psychotic one of fragmented, symbolic meanings – a treacherous first step out of foreclosure.

After a significant period of work, Mr. A was genuinely able to begin to experience feelings in association with symbolic thinking – for instance, in his use of verbal symbols to create the metaphor of the electrifying effect of "the size D batteries" in his fingers. The experience that occurred in the waiting room while Mr. A lay on the floor and I sat close to him seemed to consolidate the gains of the previous years of analytic work. Shortly after that, Mr. A began a session by speaking of his smelling the perfume and feeling the warmth of my previous patient. In contrast to his almost-exclusive reliance on foreclosure, he was now experiencing bodily sensations that felt real and that he could think about and convey in words.

In a dream that occurred in this period of the analysis, Mr. A was able for the first time to elaborate dream-thoughts in a way that went beyond "operational" thinking. In this dream, he and I were having "a conversation," and he was able to tolerate "what came up" long enough to talk and think on his own, not needing my "notes" – i.e., my thoughts as substitutes for his own. Later in the work, he experienced a thought that just "popped into" his head, about which he was able to think and dream.

Summary

I have described a patient who initially could make virtually no connection between a disturbing meeting with his boss and his panic state, nor use linking ideas that

I presented in the analysis. As the analysis progressed, the patient began to function in a fragmented state in which he was able to make use of my ideas and create connections that involved primary process and rudimentary secondary thinking, albeit connections that were fragile and that easily fell apart.

From this disorganized state in which he could begin to think thoughts and feel feelings (e.g., fear) as feelings, he progressed further to a level at which he was not only able to use verbal symbols to express personal meaning, but he could also use metaphors with transference meaning to do conscious and unconscious psychological work. Thus, initially foreclosed emotional experience that manifested itself in the form of a bodily state of panic was gradually transformed into forms of experience that could be thought, felt, spoken, remembered, and reflected upon.

Notes

1 I am using the term *panic* in a phenomenological, not a diagnostic, way – i.e., to refer to a state of intense anxiety experienced almost entirely as a bodily event, about which the person is incapable of thinking or speaking.

2 de M'Uzan uses the term *foreclosure* to refer to a form of rejection or repudiation that overshadows any of the precursors to symbolization. It is closer to Freud's (1894/1962) use of the term *verwerfung*, adapted by Lacan (1966), to describe a specific mechanism at the core of psychotic phenomena, as when De M'Uzan (2003) speaks of "the part *verwerfung* plays in hindering the constitution of the functions of symbolization, understood in the classical sense" (p. 714). The psychic disarray resulting from earlier trauma can be duplicated in an instant within the body when the body bypasses the process of symbolization, a process that would itself be so traumatic that it cannot be utilized.

3 Mr. A was referred by a behavioral therapist following unsuccessful treatment. In this way, Mr. A was following the therapist's direction for referral as well as my recommendations for treatment. His behavior in his first meeting with me involved his playing the role that he imagined a patient played with an analyst. His fantasy of what an analyst was reflected the transference he had to me before we met.

4 Second-skin formation was described by Bick (1968, 1986) as the attempt by an individual to defend against the experience of the self, which is based upon the ordering of sensory sensations at the skin surface.

5 Some years later, Bion (1987a) was more specific about the physical manifestations of beta elements when he posed the questions: "Has the parasympathetic got a brain? Does the thalamus do a parasympathetic sort of thinking?" – sounding as though these anatomical entities had "a mind of their own" (p. 253). He referred to a " 'sub-thalmic fear,' meaning the kind of fear that one would have if no check on it at all was produced by the higher levels of the mind" (Bion, 1987b, p. 319).

6 The defense of encapsulating reactions is one in which "attention has been deflected away from the objective world . . . in favor of a subjective sensation-dominated world, which is under their direct control" (Tustin, 1986, p. 25).

7 Autistic objects involve the sensory experience of a hard, angular surface created when an object is pressed against the infant's skin, which acts as a safety-generating sensory impression (Tustin, 1980).

8 Mr. A attributed to "indigestion" the events that began in his boss's office – which is how Bion refers to beta elements: "undigested or non-dreamed facts" (1962/1977, p. 7) or "objects compounded of things-in-themselves . . ." (Bion, 1963/1984, p. 40). Central to Bion's (1962/1977) thinking is the idea that, when an emotional experience is not transformed by alpha function into symbolic representations that can be used in dreaming, thinking,

and remembering, there is no alternative to evacuating these "accretions of stimuli" (beta elements) in the form of hallucination, excessive projective identification, psychosomatic disorders, or beta screens (anticommunication).

9 Bion (1990) wrote, "But it is not all a matter of 'words.' In fact, what a child picks up is not in 'verbal' form; it is infra-verbal, ultra-verbal, pre-verbal, post-verbal. There is no way of describing what sort of verbal it is. This language is communicated by . . . something which is not words" (p. 149).

10 Bion's (1962/1977) concept of the container-contained addresses "not what we think, but the way we think, that is, how we process lived experience and what occurs psychically when we are unable to do psychological work with that experience" (Ogden, 2004a, p. 1354; see also Ogden, 2004b; Schneider, 2003, 2005b).

11 Freud's *actual neurosis* represents the ancestor of the nosological entity of *panic*. An actual neurosis was considered to be without symbolic meaning, not amenable to analytic treatment, and believed by Freud to be a reaction to actual, everyday tension, rather than related to sexual conflict occurring from early childhood on. As it is now used, *actual neurosis* is unmediated symbolically from the body "so that 'actual' connotes the absence of the mediations which are to be encountered in the symptom-formation of the psychoneurosis" (p. 10). "The origin of the actual neurosis is not to be found in infantile conflicts, but in the present" (Laplanche & Pontalis, 1973, p. 10).

References

Bick, E. (1968). The experience of the skin in early object relations. *International Journal of Psychoanalysis*, *49*, 484–486.

Bick, E. (1986). Further considerations on the function of the skin in early object relations. *British Journal of Psychotherapy*, *2*, 292–299.

Bion, W. R. (1959). *Experiences in groups*. Basic Books.

Bion, W. R. (1977). Learning from experience. In *Seven servants*. Aronson. (Original work published 1962)

Bion, W. R. (1984). *Elements of psychoanalysis*. Karnac Books. (Original work published 1963)

Bion, W. R. (1987a). Four discussions. In F. Bion (Ed.), *Clinical seminars and other works*. Karnac Books.

Bion, W. R. (1987b). Four papers. In F. Bion (Ed.), *Clinical seminars and other works*. Karnac Books.

Bion, W. R. (1990). *Brazilian lectures: 1973 São Paulo, 1974 Rio de Janeiro/São Paulo*. Karnac Books.

De M'Uzan, M. (2003). Slaves of quantity. *Psychoanalytic Quarterly*, *72*, 711–725.

Freud, S. (1962). The neuro-psychoses of defense. In J. Strachey (Ed. & Trans.), *Standard edition of the complete psychological works of Sigmund Freud* (Vol. 3, pp. 43–61). Hogarth Press. (Original work published 1894)

Grotstein, J. S. (2000). *Who is the dreamer and who dreams the dream?* Analytic Press.

Lacan, J. (1966). *Ecrits*. Seuil.

Laplanche, J., & Pontalis, J. B. (1973). *The language of psychoanalysis*. Karnac Books.

McDougall, J. (1974). The psychosoma and the psychoanalytic process. *International Review of Psychoanalysis*, *1*, 437–459.

McDougall, J. (1984). The "dis-affected" patient: reflections on affect pathology. *Psychoanalytic Quarterly*, *52*, 386–409.

McDougall, J. (1989). *Theaters of the body: A psychoanalytic approach to psychosomatic illness*. W. W. Norton.

Nemiah, J., & Sifneos, P. (1970). Affect and fantasy in patients with psychosomatic disorders. In *Modern trends in psychiatric medicine* (Vol. 2). Butterworth.

Ogden, T. (1982). *Projection, identification, and psychotherapeutic technique*. Aronson.

Ogden, T. (1989). *The primitive edge of experience*. Aronson/Karnac Books.

Ogden, T. (2004a). On holding and containing, being and dreaming. *International Journal of Psychoanalysis, 85*, 1349–1364.

Ogden, T. (2004b). This art of psychoanalysis: dreaming undreamt dreams and interrupted cries. *International Journal of Psychoanalysis, 85*, 857–877.

Schneider, J. A. (2003). Janus-faced resilience in the analysis of a severely traumatized patient. *Psychoanalytic Review, 90*(6), 869–887.

Schneider, J. A. (2005a). Experiences in K and –K. *International Journal of Psychoanalysis, 86*, 825–839.

Schneider, J. A. (2005b). Dreaming the truth of experience: "Heaven." *Psychoanalytic Review, 92*(5), 777–785.

Tustin, F. (1980). Autistic objects. *International Review of Psychoanalysis, 7*, 27–40.

Tustin, F. (1981). *Autistic states in children*. Routledge/Kegan Paul.

Tustin, F. (1986). *Autistic barriers in neurotic patients*. Yale University Press.

Tustin, F. (1990). *The protective shell in children and adults*. Karnac Books.

5

Working With Pathological and Healthy Forms of Splitting

It has increasingly seemed to me over the years that difficulties arise in analytic work with borderline and other seriously disturbed patients when the analyst fails to distinguish pathological splitting from healthy, but immature, forms of splitting.[1] Healthy, primitive splitting represents an important developmental step, serving as a transition into more richly human forms of defense and communication/expression, and as a powerful precursor of (and always-present facet of) ambivalence and mature integration of self.[2]

A possibility I propose is that because of its polarizing effect, splitting creates a generative space in which contrasts can be brought into relationship with one another in imagination. By taking things apart and keeping the two sides separate, one avoids a defensive and premature closure. This keeps open a clearance for something new to happen from the tension created between the two sides, as found in ambivalence, and regaining parts of the self, or facing intolerable anxieties. In pathological splitting, no space is opened through symbolization for consolidation of disparate elements. In healthy splitting, things can be freshly thought about and new thoughts generated, thus allowing for a mental playfulness such as in metaphor.

In this article, I offer a case discussion in which it was necessary for me to distinguish pathological splitting from healthy (albeit, primitive) splitting in order for me to become able to speak with the patient in a way that allowed us to traverse an analytic impasse.

I am well aware of the importance of splitting as a defense – as a specific mental activity designed to protect an individual against thoughts and feelings that are experienced as dangerously at odds with one another. I also understand splitting as a way of organizing experience.[3] In the human world, the infant uses splitting to separate the good breast/mother from the bad breast/mother. For the infant, the good object/breast is loved and valued instinctively for the functions and safety it supplies. This instinctual splitting creates order and safety at the level of signal functioning, devoid of symbolic (interpretive) meaning.[4] Optimally, the mother provides everything needed by the infant, thus allowing an interpretive space to open in which primitive symbolic communication can begin to take place.

I think of splitting not only as a pathological process antithetical to integration, but also, and more importantly, as a preparatory process. Splitting is part of a healthy

DOI:10.4324/9781003384601-5

continuum of ways we relate aspects of ourselves to one another, and ways we defensively urge others to live out aspects of ourselves and our roles.

I

Clinical Illustration

I will present portions of an analysis of a patient who relied heavily on splitting and who taught me a good deal about the subtle differences among a variety of forms of splitting. The fragment of the analysis is taken from the middle of the 8th year of a four-sessions-per-week analysis in which the patient, Ms. N, used the couch. Ms. N was a 58-year-old married woman who had three grown children. She was born in Europe and raised in a small town on the East Coast of the United States. During our work together, she was employed as a highly paid administrator in an advertising agency.

Initial Stagnation

I will begin by focusing on a recent period of analysis in which something puzzling – at times startling – was occurring. These particular sessions stand out because they are at the cusp of a change, a change that was not fortuitous, but came as a result of psychoanalytic work that allowed splitting to become less adversarial and paralyzing in foreclosing thoughts about what was happening in the experience of splitting.

For several weeks, Ms. N was inexplicably enraged with me, more so than ever before – and she had often been furious with me. Ms. N, in this period, gave me the impression that I was causing her unrelenting pain and hell, approaching the level of torture. In her rage, she endlessly devalued me and my attempts to understand what had taken place that may have led to such anger. She felt completely justified in her vitriolic attacks on me and wondered how she had ever allowed herself to trust me. At times she felt that she had, in fact, known all along that I would ultimately fail her, and had hidden that awareness from herself. All the history we shared was wiped out or rewritten. I found myself feeling that she was treating me like a completely new person – one whom I did not recognize as myself.

Before the onset of this rage, our work seemed to have been moving toward a sense of connection, accomplishment, and understanding of one another. But in this period of extreme rage, I experienced profound self-doubt and wondered if I had missed something important in our work. I attempted to look at what might have caused such an extreme and rapid swing of feeling.

I was reminded that in our initial sessions, Ms. N had idolized me. She let me know I was for her all that was good, and that she felt unworthy to be in my presence and undeserving to be treated by me in analysis. At times our meetings took on a quasi-religious quality. In one session, she turned me into a Christ-like figure when backlighting from the window behind my chair led her to see me with a shroud surrounded by a halo. Ms. N's eloquent adulation did not feel flattering or comfortable;

rather, the idealization made me feel unreal, nonexistent, a parody of my real self. It seemed to me that this exaggerated praise was an unconscious way of communicating how unsafe and unreal she felt and what a fall she anticipated. She was showing me in this what was for her a fact of life: What you see is not what you get. At the same time as Ms. N idolized me, she denigrated herself.

In a session several months into the analysis, Ms. N showed me bruises on her body and told me how, when she threatened to leave her husband, he pinned her against the garage with the family car. I was startled by the degree to which Ms. N was able to use pathological splitting. It did not seem at all odd to her that she could calmly return home each evening to her violent, psychotic spouse, who several times had come close to killing her.

Ms. N could so disconnect aspects of her conscious and unconscious experience that she could nonchalantly deny having felt anger toward me in sessions immediately after she had been raging at me. I found this profoundly confusing and disturbing.

Ms. N's fury at me in the period I am describing reminded me of the grueling battles she engaged in with her mother when she was a child. One battle that came to mind involved a struggle about her picking up her room. One day as she was leaving for school, her mother offered to tidy up her room, explaining that Ms. N's friend was coming over to play after school, and that the patient would, of course, want her things in order. When Ms. N arrived home with her friend, she found her room in shambles. Her mother had swept through the room like a cyclone – emptying all the drawers and closets, stripping the bed and walls, and piling everything in a heap on the floor.

On another occasion, when Ms. N was going to her first dance in grade school, her mother offered to help her with her hair. Her mother asked Ms. N to get her a chair to stand on so she could reach the top of Ms. N's head (her mother was much shorter than Ms. N).

After getting on the chair, Ms. N's mother started slapping Ms. N's face and pulling her hair out because of her rage over a note she had found detailing a rendezvous Ms. N had planned with friends after the dance.

Ms. N's father never intervened in these battles. The patient described him as impotent and ineffectual. In the scene, both as originally experienced by the patient and as represented in the transference-countertransference, the patient's father was present in his absence. Her mother's hatred – experienced by Ms. N as her own in the transference – was undiluted by a protective paternal transference experience. I hypothesized silently that Ms. N's denial of her current rage at me involved a form of projective identification in which I experienced some of the patient's confusion about her mother's psychotic, disavowed anger at her.

From the beginning of the analysis, Ms. N relied on several pathological forms of splitting to keep me from getting inside of her and to protect herself from the dangers she felt I posed. She used headphones and earplugs, and stuck her fingers in her ears to keep me out and to keep at a distance the dangerous parts of herself that she had (in unconscious fantasy) projected into me. In our sessions, she variously wore sunglasses, kept her eyes squeezed shut, repeatedly took her glasses off and on, or "forgot" her glasses so she could not see.

In so doing, Ms. N, in fantasy, was able to eject and not let back in all dangerous sounds and dangerous thoughts such as anger, madness, amorphous terrors, murderous thoughts, and sexual excitement. In these sessions, she projected the dangerous feelings or parts of her self into me so she would no longer feel at war with herself and, in the process of disintegrating, could, instead, feel at war with me and held together in me. In this way, my "affective resonance" (Hoffman, 1992) was critical to my thinking and experiencing.

I wondered if all our work had been for nothing. My fear that our work was over was accompanied by humiliating images of the two of us going before a mediator to work things out. The mediator perhaps signified my feeling that I could not regain a sense of the analytic space and my own integrity as an analyst without a third person (albeit a sternly judgmental one) to replace what seemed to have been lost in me and between us.

Analytic Roles Cast in Concrete

My anxiety about Ms. N's raging at me led me to consider a variety of theoretical frameworks in an attempt to return to solid ground, including Bion's (1957/1967) version of projective identification, Ogden's (1994) concept of the analytic third, and Hoffman's (1992) notion of social constructivism. As I became aware of my efforts to rely on the ideas of others to replace my own thoughts, feelings, and perceptions, I felt greater confidence in my own capacity for thinking. I realized that Ms. N was unconsciously, in a sadistic and rageful way, leading me to be unable to think. I said to her,

> I think you must feel despairing that I'll ever understand you and so you feel you have to show me what it feels like to be you – to feel worthless, to be hounded by self-doubt and hopelessness – even to be robbed of the ability to think.

Practically before I had finished speaking, Ms. N launched into a tirade, attacking me for getting it wrong. I sensed that her accusations were leveled at me for not being the idealized good, loving mother, and, instead, being a mother who, because of her confusing, frightening unreliability, had to be omnipotently controlled.

I felt compelled to address the isolating effect of her defensive outrage at the failure of her omnipotence to fully control me – in this instance, by ignoring or twisting my interpretations. I told her:

> I can imagine that this is something that may have happened thousands of times with your mother, your sisters, and your husband; and so it's natural that you would expect it of me. I think that your battering me in this way may be an attempt to get me to loosen my grip on what I think I know and on who I am for myself as an analyst, and to pull me into something I can't possibly figure out because there

is no rhyme or reason to it. I think you're trying to recreate with me the experience you had of being pulled into their craziness and of not being able to prevent losing yourself in them.

The patient seemed to calm down a little bit in response to these interpretations. Later in that meeting, I ended a period of sustained silence by saying:

> You and I have worked together long enough and hard enough to know that this is not a contemplative silence but a turning your nose up at me while appearing not to be doing so. I think you're trying to induce in me the anger you're unable to bear. I have an idea that your aim is to get me to feel the helpless, out-of-control feelings you felt as a child and are finding unbearable now. Holding a grudge against me for crimes neither of us can fully name allows you not to risk a relationship with me in the present; everything is sealed in a death grip. You pay for this with a feeling of terrible isolation.

When she responded a few minutes later, she said:

> That's your language of "death grip" and "grudge." No way it is for me, and I'm trying to step back and lend a sense of understanding for what is going on here. And I appreciate it doesn't ring true for you. I'm very aware of the repetitive nature of this experience. I've thought too hard and worked too hard not to see the confusion of many similar experiences with my mother, sisters, father, and with you. I appreciate that, and I understand that sometimes. This isn't that. And if anything, I am terrifically anxious to move past that. I wish this were a reenactment and not something just between us.

I could feel in a visceral way Ms. N's confusion and her sense of losing herself, which were communicated in part through her imitation of the sound of my voice and her use of words that were the same as or similar to mine (e.g., "thought too hard and worked too hard," "lend a sense of understanding," and "ring true.") I also experienced the last part of her response as particularly clipped, almost staccato-like. I was reminded of studying my first piano piece that called for staccato and trying to make each note sharper, shorter, and more distinct from the others while still maintaining the melody. I went on to say:

> I think that when you begin to feel you're losing yourself in me and my words, you try as best you can to separate yourself from me. I think you try to do this separating by experiencing me and my ideas as having nothing to do with you, which leaves you entirely on your own. It's almost as if you feel there's a 6-inch Plexiglass screen between the two of us with nothing passing through.

Later in that meeting, I repeated that she must believe loneliness is an acceptable price to pay because it protects her from feeling either utterly helpless and isolated in the face of my failing to understand, or feeling taken over by my ideas and by my efforts to make her part of me. I suggested that in her state of mind, what seemed like a refusal to learn was actually her effort to protect herself against being taken over by me. I told her I thought that she must feel an ever-present danger of someone or something – like a virus or bacterium – taking her over and running things their way.

She responded in a high-pitched, child-like voice (the opposite of mine, I thought) as she forced a cheerful smile and said: "Oh, um, your words make sense." From her tone of voice, I could tell that she could not hear or felt compelled to negate what I was saying in the form I was putting it. Her response seemed to be the opposite of me or what I experienced as the truth – certainly in terms of rational organization of ideas, feelings, and sensations.

As she spoke, I had the impression that, for her, words were empty, just weapons in disguise – and that she felt contempt for spoken words as cynical manipulations of the listener. I had the feeling that she was simply mouthing words, like a cow absently chewing her cud.

It was only after the session that I became aware of the disguised anger in my accusatory interpretation concerning Ms. N's battering me as well as my silently comparing her to a cow chewing her cud. I again wondered whether her using some of my words might have reflected her having experienced me as having mouthed others' words and ideas (e.g., those of Bion (1957/1967), Klein (1935/1968), Ogden (1994), and Winnicott (1971).

With this growing self-awareness, I was able to decrease my defensive use of the theoretical frameworks of others and begin thinking for myself. I was then better able to experience more of the intensity and complexity of what was going on between us. I could begin to reflect on my identification with Ms. N in her sense of failure, despair, and isolation. Only then did I realize that her controlling efforts reflected unbearable anxiety. My fuller recognition of my anger allowed a shift in me such that I was able to feel a deeper sense of compassion for Ms. N of which I had previously been incapable. I could hear as well as feel (in a sensory way) the change in the sound of my voice.

I acknowledged to myself that she had, in fact, made some movement toward a different form of splitting. I remembered when she told me that initially she experienced me as aspects of "50 songs" pieced together, with no semblance of wholeness, and that this experience changed from day to day. Then, over time, she said I had become a single person, and that now she had only one "version" of me, one person 50 years old.

A Reflecting Space Recognizing the Analytic Situation

Several sessions later, Ms. N seemed to make a pivotal movement from her previous, hostile state. Initially I did not know how to respond. She told me she had attended a symphony performance during which she had reflected on what had been taking place between us.

When I don't understand a musical piece, my first idea is to ask what does it feel like, what is it that feels threatening about the music. On Saturday night, I realized the piece seemed weak. In the past, I'd just turn it off mentally and not hear it. But analysis has taught me to stay with it and try to understand it, so I've learned to turn up the volume so I can hear it better. It's like images not so clear or understandable in dreams. Analysis has taught me that my stumbling block to understanding is not limited by my intelligence but by something else about me.

That was when that moment I was waiting for happened to me. It clicked on – the light had been off for weeks. This has happened in major work times here – the light goes on. All of a sudden I see and understand. Without faith in our analytic work, I wouldn't be lying here with the capacity to experience the work before me – like having been in the dark and switching the light on and seeing. I doubted myself, so I became extremely discontented with my ability to think and understand. I felt completely lost because I doubted myself so severely that I couldn't be a vessel for treatment, for understanding.

I was part of the music on Saturday – I can't overstate it – especially the Brahms First Symphony. I knew every note. So having had the door opened – and in a place that involves music I love – there was just no way to take you out of those experiences even though you weren't there. In a way, this work has taught me to think – I could not be there if I hadn't taken my place. That's why it's so powerful.

As I listened, I found her response intriguing, but I was aware of how forced and almost magical it seemed, perhaps reflecting a manic defense[5] in response to anxiety about loss of omnipotent control over me and the rest of the world, which would leave her absolutely alone.

I was also aware that her referring to herself as a "vessel" of treatment was a very passive way of putting it; it seemed submissive and a reassertion of at-oneness with me. Her referring to the analysis as "this work" seemed removed, mechanical, and impersonal. It seemed to me that her apparent epiphany was at best an important first step toward whole and separate object relatedness.

As I thought about it, I realized that this new development in Ms. N's sense of making our work understandable differed from prior shifts in several ways. Previously she had taken in, reworked, and automatically accepted my interpretation of events while in my office, swallowing the whole of it undigested, using my words, as if my interpretation were a sticky glue pad to hold pieces of her self together to give the appearance of wholeness.

This time her understanding came about by way of a more considered, albeit somewhat hypomanic, response that involved a new version of our relationship that included both of us. It seemed important that she had arrived at these ideas outside the office, in a state of reverie at the symphony. It seemed that her reverie added a third term to our relationship, a beginning of a thinking and interpreting self. She could begin to "talk to herself" in a meaningful way (with me as an imagined presence).

Ms. N's ability to create a working metaphor for our relationship contributed to the creation of a symbolizing space (Winnicott, 1971 "play space"). In that "analytic space" (Ogden, 1994) between us, we could begin to think for ourselves and talk to each other as separate people.

In the next meeting, she reflected on what had transpired between us, saying:

> In the exact moment you asked what the experience at the symphony was like for me, the image immediately came to my head of a ball going into a mitt. It's just effortless the way you catch a ball – it's so simple, yet so powerful. Of course it's part of a bigger play. But at the moment when it's in play, the only action is of the ball to the glove – a receptive place fits the ball to the glove. For a moment nothing is more valuable, more real, than the ball finding its place in the mitt. It's in play more than anything else on the diamond. At the moment, I'm in the game – a perfect moment. [The patient did not know consciously that from childhood one of my great pleasures in life has been baseball.]

Ms. N's response about play was the beginning of play itself. Her use of language here, as in poetry, was not about an event – it was the event. Though her words were about baseball, the alive event in the hour was her genuinely creative, metaphoric use of language.[6]

A few months later, a session occurred in which we experienced an unusually intense sense of closeness and intimacy. I was aware of speaking haltingly and recasting my thoughts as I spoke. Ms. N told me she had realized something that had surprised her. In previous meetings, when she had been confused and anxious, she would resolve to be more organized and purposeful between the meetings and at the next meeting. She told me that when earlier in the session she felt confused, she found herself feeling closer and more connected to me. She now realized that, for her, being purposeful and organized was characterized by thinking, not feeling; so when she attempted to be purposeful and organized, she actually felt more distant than when she experienced some confusion. (From the perspective being developed in this article, I understood her "organized" state as a defensive premature organization of experience in the form of pathological splitting.)

Thoughtfully, Ms. N went on to say that in addition to how and what we were talking about, she experienced my halting speech as giving rise to a depth of closeness – a feeling of being understood in a way she had not previously been able to feel with me. At this point, I said to Ms. N, "What you're describing about your experience and feelings here today is something that you couldn't have done a year or even 6 months ago."

I am aware at times of greater connection, of being more thoughtful which is reflected in my choice of words, tone of voice, and rhythm of speaking. I thought Ms. N might have been responding also to my less blaming and alienating thoughts. I agreed with her observation that the tentative, halting quality of my speech reflected a feeling state that stood in contrast to a ready, knowing interpretation. In this way it seemed to allow an openness on her part as well as my own for collaborative adjustments in what was being put into words. This experience of putting our feelings and thoughts into words had a highly personal feel to both of us.

The change in my tone came as I gained distance from my experience instead of being immersed in it. I had been participating in the interactions before thinking, but with the space that opened up between us (although it took some time), I was better able to begin an internal narrative. I was able to step out of the experience of the projective identification sufficiently to symbolize and talk to myself and eventually to Ms. N about what I had been experiencing. This allowed me to not only speak about the experience but also to speak from it.

When I met Ms. N in the waiting room for our next session, I was immediately aware that she was wearing a pleasantly sweet perfume. I did not recall her ever having worn perfume and thought that this might be a response to what had occurred in our last session. This meeting in the waiting room had something of the feel of a date.

A dream I had over the weekend may also have contributed to how I was responding to Ms. N. In the dream, I felt uninhibited about deep, pleasurable erotic sensations that fully permeated my body. On awakening, I realized to my surprise that my sexual aliveness in the dream was connected to my recent experiences in the work with Ms. N. I came to experience the dream as a freeing experience – an indication that I was working on this unconsciously.

The patient began the session by telling me that she had a dream in which she was at a hospitality suite in a major hotel. She was there to receive an important award for her job performance and to accept a promotion. She was at the podium about to give her acceptance speech when she noticed me walking into the room with a female colleague. She was shocked and wondered what I was doing with that floozy. She felt sad and upset that I was with a woman known for her flirtatious nature and promiscuous sexual activity, which ended each time in the man's being hurt. She watched me as I mingled with the crowd, whereupon she lost sight of me.

Ms. N said that she thought the dream was a response to our last session, but parts of it did not fit. She found herself in the familiar process of getting caught up and lost in the good and satisfying feelings, and then quickly changing her focus to bittersweet and bad feelings. She felt she was responsible for my being with this woman in the dream and was sad that she was moving on in her career and leaving me with someone like this woman.

The patient went on to say that she was also angry with me. Why was I with this woman? Was there something she had missed in her perception of me? Her questions made her aware that she was jettisoning her more satisfying feelings. She then wondered, "Of all the people in the world to have in the dream, why this woman?" I commented somewhat reflexively that the dream was her dream, and she was the playwright and director who had placed the various characters in the dream, including pairing me with the other woman. Almost immediately I realized that what I had said sounded sour and defensive, perhaps as an anxious response to the fact that as playwright and director, *I* had put her in *my* dream.

Ms. N said she had been frightened about openly expressing her feelings of attraction toward me, afraid I might reject her, that I might even be angered. She then wondered whether pairing me with the "floozy" might be a way for her indirectly to be with me – that is, by both disguising herself and by demeaning herself and the experience.

Discussion

Movement toward experiencing oneself as a whole and separate person is never a straight line and commonly proceeds in fits and starts in a back-and-forth fashion. We optimally achieve a dialectic tension of mature ambivalence and healthy but primitive splitting, each negating and preserving one another. Static wholeness is opposed by the opening up of closures (healthy splitting), thus allowing something new to occur in a person's psychological life (Bion, 1962a, 1963; Eigen, 1985; Ogden, 1988).

It was an achievement for Ms. N to move from a largely chaotic internal world to a more ordered one organized by means of splitting. The clinical work just presented involved an effort to help the patient progress beyond an initial unconscious reliance on pathological splitting that had resulted in a defensive psychological closure and a stagnation of the analysis.

Because of the difficulties in the countertransference, I did not sufficiently acknowledge (nor was I sufficiently aware of) the small but significant advances that Ms. N had made in the direction of primitive healthy splitting. The countertransference difficulties I experienced (feeling confused, powerless, and angry) led me to be unreceptive to Ms. N's maturation. I gradually became aware of the potential for anger on both our parts to lock us into a stalemate based on a polarization: I felt she was a recalcitrant patient; she felt I was a stubborn analyst.

The result was a polarization based on pathological splitting enacted in the transference/countertransference. This petrified polarization might have gone on for the duration of the analysis because a distinguishing feature of pathological splitting is that it does not go anywhere; there is no communication among the unconsciously split-off elements of the patient. This static pathological organization based on splitting results in a polarized transference-countertransference that allows us little if any room for genuine communication or psychological change.

Ms. N had treated me for years as a part-object by incessantly speaking "at me" in rapid fire; during that period, I had felt scattered and confused, at times bored and sleepy, at times nauseous and unreal. Only later did I come to understand that her incessant talking and barraging me with seemingly inconsequential details represented her need to be known by me "in all her bits and pieces" (see Winnicott, 1945/1975, p. 150).[7]

Ms. N's traumatic experiences with her mother – the mother's unexpected switching from a seemingly comforting person to a humiliating and terrifying force – were initially brought to the analysis in the form of sensations in and on the body (e.g., my feeling nauseous and sleepy) and of having her inside on the outside. Her mother's emptying the contents of her drawers onto the floor (symbolically exposing Ms. N's private parts) – turning inside into outside – humiliated Ms. N. It not only betrayed the patient's privacy but also – because the act was viewed by her friend – humiliated Ms. N by exposing her family's psychotic qualities.

Ms. N had no words for her terror: As a child she was forbidden to put feelings into words, and she had complied both in her spoken words and in her thoughts. Ms.

N evoked in me feelings similar to those she experienced with her mother, and she enlisted me in the unconscious experiencing of anger and fear like her own.

It was essential for me to recognize Ms. N's further movement toward generative splitting, as she created a form of communication between formerly split-off aspects of herself (enacted in the polarized transference-countertransference). There was an ongoing danger of my slipping back into defensive anger so as not to be drawn in by her and lose myself in her. For example, I was overly skeptical of her symphony response, feeling it was brittle and overdone.

Without her realizing it, Ms. N's state of reverie at the symphony had been a metaphor for what occurred when a "symphony" occurred in her. *Symphony* is a word with roots in Greek: *phonic* – meaning related to sounds and symbols, and *sym* – meaning a bringing together, as a number of instruments or a set of symbolic elements might come together as something larger than the sum of its parts. Her symphony generatively brought together parts of herself, at least temporarily. The symphonic sounds would not be worth anything unless there was someone to hear them as music (and not simply as a group of musical notes) (Laplance, and Pontalis,1967)[8].

It seems to me now, on the basis of the understandings discussed thus far, that there were several primary factors leading to Ms. N's reverie at the symphony. My use of countertransference analysis (including my analytic use of my reverie experience) allowed me to gain a better sense of the nature of the impasse. For example, I became aware that the metaphor comparing the patient to a cow chewing her cud reflected unanalyzed anger in the countertransference. By refocusing my attention on the cud metaphor, I was able to shift to a more empathic reflection. I acknowledged to myself and to Ms. N the progress in her experience of me as a whole person instead of parts of 50 ever-changing songs. My recognition of my anger and frustration and resultant softening of my words and voice allowed room for Ms. N's shift in her unconscious feeling state. She moved from more defensive "thinking" to feelings that felt real to her.

What was essential in this sequence was my ability to be sufficiently conversant with my own conscious and unconscious anger to recognize and acknowledge even very small movements on the patient's part toward more generative splitting (i.e., splitting that allowed at least some enriching discourse between the disconnected elements).

I came to understand how her response to the symphony was directly related to the shift in me. It also became clear to me that I had missed something genuinely new in her symphony metaphor and instead dismissed the experience and the metaphor as a forced, overdone testimonial.

Ms. N's awareness of her own role in the polarization further facilitated development of a more mature, generative splitting that formed the basis for ambivalence and other forms of mature, complex psychological divisions (which never "outgrow" splitting). As her capacity to split developed, differences became clearer, and charged with affect other than fear, and were even welcomed with interest and curiosity.

Ms. N was much less defensive – due to unconscious feedback loops, and a dampening of her characteristic immediate kindling response, which had previously led to physical reactions that settled in and produced a background of static to any clear communication. At this point in the treatment, she could interrupt this feedback loop at its inception before physical reactions occurred.

By our repeatedly re-working these themes, Ms. N made more conspicuous shifts. I, in turn, was able much more fully to acknowledge the changes that had occurred in the analytic relationship: the shift in the polarization/splitting of our relationship as I became able to be more thoughtful (e.g., as I spoke haltingly instead of offering pre-fabricated generic interpretations). This joint effort to create something genuinely new was paradoxically an experience in which we were able to psychically disentangle ourselves from one another.

The analytic process I have described involved the interplay of conscious and un-conscious states of reverie of analyst and analysand as described by Bion (1962b) and Ogden (1997). The dreams – Ms. N's and mine – were a continuation of the predomi-nant themes of transference-countertransference left unresolved in the previous session (Boyer, 1988). We were unconsciously in conversation with each other, which we reg-istered by our dreams. I was able to appreciate Ms. N as a woman and have a physical experience of her in my dream that was sensual but not perverse. The two dreams felt like two halves of the same symbolic work.

Ms. N's dream involved an effort both to disguise her feelings and to reveal them to me and to herself. My own dream seemed both integrative and discriminating in that the dream confirmed a sexual aliveness being experienced by us for the first time in relation to one another while stopping short of incestuous mergers (which would have felt frightening, "creepy," and out of control). To both Ms. N and me, the "other woman" seemed to be Ms. N in a disavowed, denigrated form which she used to distance herself from her own loving/sexual feelings toward me and to defend herself against her fears of rejection.

Concluding Comments

In thinking about the analytic work with Ms. N, I would suggest several ideas that may be generalizable to other clinical work.

First is the importance of awareness of the potential for anger in the transference–countertransference to lock patient and analyst in a stalemated polarization in which each experiences the other as obtuse, selfish, sadistic, insincere, mechanical, and so on. Under such circumstances, the therapist may be slow and reluctant to recognize genuine change or sincere effort on the part of the patient; what change is recognized by the analyst is likely to be undervalued.

Second, countertransference analysis – including the therapist's analytic use of his or her dreams and reveries – may lead to the analyst's gaining a sense of the nature of the unconscious splitting process underlying the impasse in the analysis. This, in turn, may lead to a shift in the analyst's participation in the pathological splitting going on in the analytic relationship. In my work with Ms. N, my awareness that comparing her in metaphor to a cow chewing her cud reflected my coming to terms with unanalyzed anger in the countertransference. This led to the beginning of the creation of a reflec-tive space, a clearance in which to think.

Third, the analyst, having become aware of his or her own conscious and uncon-scious anger, is better able to recognize, acknowledge, and appreciate even the simplest and most unimpressive changes toward healthy splitting. Healthy, primitive splitting often takes the form, as it did with Ms. N, of the beginnings of the creation of a generative space between formerly disconnected feeling states and aspects of self in which some communication among them can begin to take place. Experientially, this psychological shift has the feeling of the creation of a clearance in which thinking, meaningful discriminations, and mutually understanding conversations between patient and analyst can occur. In this analytic case, splitting led to what seemed to be the patient's eventual use of un-self-consciously creative metaphors to communicate her experience in verbally symbolic form.

Fourth, the analyst, having recognized the patient's movement toward generative splitting, is liable to slip back into defensive responses to the patient so as not to be "taken in" metaphorically and concretely (in fantasy) by the patient. In the analysis of Ms. N, I was overly skeptical of her account of the symphony. It was, in fact, brittle and overdone, but I was still too angry to recognize or acknowledge the healthy change it reflected.

In the course of an analysis, as during infant development, the analyst plays an important role in mediating movement from primitive persecutory phantasies to more alive forms of symbolization. Only in this way is it possible for one to learn from experience and to eventually achieve capacities for empathy for others and responsibility for oneself.

Notes

1   Pruyser (1975) and Grotstein (1985) provide a comprehensive overview of splitting.
2   Klein (1946/1975) developed Freud's paradigm of splitting, which he presented in his paper on fetishism (1926/1961) and further spelled out in another paper (1933/1964). Klein saw splitting as part of the pathology of infantile psychosis, and thus as a primitive defense used to manage danger posed by the threat of internal destructiveness. When moving from the paranoid-schizoid to the depressive positions, the polar opposites of the good and bad breasts are brought closer together. One relies less heavily on splitting, and develops the capacity for ambivalence. This includes the ability to hold positive and negative feelings for the object while holding a sense of the wholeness of the object. The part not spelled out in Kline's theory is the specific way splitting is not simply brought into balance and overcome.
3   At its most basic level, splitting involves a simple binomial sorting of experiences that is similar in nature to most basic animal defense systems. The simplicity of binary processing is beneficial in terms of self-preservation as well as preservation of the species. For example, on the Serengeti Plain of Tanzania, animals make split-second decisions to fight, flee, or stay by distinguishing between danger and safety, predator and prey. Life and death hang in the balance of reaction times measured in minute fractions of a second. A binary signal system needs only to make a determination concerning the perception of danger, and does not involve the complicated, cumbersome, time-consuming decision work of interpretation.
4   At birth, infants' physiology is more advanced than their psychical processes. By separating what they cannot yet tolerate psychically and projecting it into the mother for safe-keeping – thus buying psychic time – they protect themselves from being emotionally overwhelmed.
5   The "manic defense" (Klein, 1935/1968; Schneider, 1990, 1995) is a set of primitive defenses mounted in response to depressive anxiety – one fears that one has hurt or killed a person one loves and depends on, leaving the individual painfully and helplessly alone. Manic defense involves three overlapping defensive maneuvers in relation to the object: control, contempt, and triumph. Patients relying on a manic defense unconsciously fantasize that

they omnipotently control the person they are afraid of losing. An object fully under one's control cannot leave; even if the object leaves, nothing is lost because he or she is viewed as contemptible and worthless. In fact, the loss of the object is an occasion for triumphant feelings because one is better off without it.

6   For additional reading, see Ogden (1999).

7   Ms. N had described this experience of pathologically incomplete splitting: "It's like confetti pieces on my desk looking up at me and screaming – like confetti because they are very mobile and are shifting and screaming. Not even like puzzle pieces because there's no place to interlock . . . they are very chaotic and very loud . . . at one time they were all pieces of one big piece of paper . . . these things might be put back into one big whole, 8 1/2 x 11 page."

8   The English word "symbol" is derived from a Greek word referring to an agreement or contract between two people, which was signified by breaking a stone in half. Each of the two people kept one half of the stone. The two halves uniquely fit back together and thus served to signify both the agreement and the identity of the two people who had entered into it. Each of the two halves of the stone that had been created by breaking the whole stone were not worth anything on their own. The two people had to integrate the image, to bring the two sides together in order to create meaning.

References

Bion, W. R. (1962a). A theory of thinking. *International Journal of Psychoanalysis, 43*, 4–5.

Bion, W. R. (1962b). *Learning from experience*. Basic Books.

Bion, W. R. (1963). *Elements of psychoanalysis*. Heinemann.

Bion, W. R. (1967). Differentiation of the psychotic from the non-psychotic personalities. In *Second thoughts* (pp. 43–64). Jason Aronson. (Original work published 1957)

Boyer, L. B. (1988). Thinking of the interview as if it were a dream. *Contemporary Psychoanalysis, 24*, 275–281.

Eigen, M. (1985). Toward Bion's starting point: Between catastrophe and faith. *International Journal of Psychoanalysis, 66*, 321–330.

Freud, S. (1961). Fetishism. In J. Strachey (Ed. & Trans.), *Standard edition of the complete psychological works of Sigmund Freud* (Vol. 21, pp. 147–157). Hogarth Press. (Original work published 1926)

Freud, S. (1964). New introductory lectures on psychoanalysis. In J. Strachey (Ed. & Trans.), *Standard edition of the complete psychological works of Sigmund Freud* (Vol. 22, pp. 1–182). Hogarth Press. (Original work published 1933)

Grotstein, J. S. (1985). *Splitting and projective identification*. Jason Aronson.

Hoffman, I. (1992). Some practical implications of a social-constructivist view of the psychoanalytic situation. *Psychoanalytic Dialogues: A Journal of Relational Perspectives, 2*, 287–304.

Klein, M. (1968). A contribution to the psychogenesis of manic-depressive states. In *Contributions to psychoanalysis 1921–1945* (pp. 282–311). Hogarth Press. (Original work published 1935)

Klein, M. (1975). Notes on some schizoid mechanisms. In *Envy and gratitude and other works, 1946–1963* (pp. 24–42). Delacorte. (Original work published 1946)

Laplanche, J., & Pontalis, J. B. (1967). *The language of Psyco-Analysis*. Trans. D. Nicholson-Smith. New York: W.W. Norton, 1973.

Ogden, T. (1988). On the dialectical structure of experience: Some clinical and theoretical implications. *Contemporary Psychoanalysis, 24*, 17–45.

Ogden, T. (1994). *Subjects of analysis*. Jason Aronson.

Ogden, T. (1997). *Reverie and interpretation: Sensing something human*. Jason Aronson.

Ogden, T. (1999). "The music of what happens" in poetry and psychoanalysis. *International Journal of Psychoanalysis, 80*, 979–994.

Pruyser, P. (1975). What splits in 'splitting'? A scrutiny of the concepts of splitting in psychoanalysis and psychiatry. *Bulletin of the Menninger Clinic, 39*, 1–46.

Schneider, J. A. (1990). Gender identity issues in male bulimia nervosa. In C. Johnson (Ed.), *Psychodynamic treatment of anorexia nervosa and bulimia* (pp. 194–222). Guilford Press.

Schneider, J. A. (1995). Eating disorders, addictions, and unconscious fantasy. *Bulletin of the Menninger Clinic, 59*(2), 177–199.

Winnicott, D. W. (1971). *Playing and reality*. Basic Books.

Winnicott, D. W. (1975). Primitive emotional development. In *Through paediatrics to psychoanalysis* (pp. 145–156). Basic Books. (Original work published 1945)

6

Experiences in K and −K

The central aim of psychoanalysis is to make the undreamable dreamable, and the unthinkable thinkable. Both patient and analyst are continuously adjusting their need to know and their need not to know as they attempt to render coherent the incoherent. Critical to this endeavor is the development of the capacity of the analyst and patient to tolerate doubt as they attempt to live with painful emotional experience.

In this chapter, I consider ideas related to Bion's conception of the human need *to get to know* (K), the "truth instinct" (Grotstein (2004, p. 104). My focus is on both K and the equally important quality, "the need not to know, not to learn, not to understand," which Bion designates −K. K is a process of getting to know, and −K is an undermining of that process (mis-knowing, misrepresenting, misunderstanding) − whether it be a person, a feeling, or a thought.[1] I will discuss varieties of K and −K as elements of a healthy titration of knowing and not knowing.

Bion discusses −K in terms of "one factor only − envy" (1962, p. 96). He acknowledges that his doing so represents a highly incomplete study of −K and implies that his understanding of −K goes far beyond envy as its only, or even its primary, motivating force. I will address manifestations of −K not driven by envy and, consequently, not necessarily pathological or pathogenic. What I am focusing upon is the way in which −K can be put to use by the personality, particularly the non-psychotic aspect of the personality (Bion, 1965), as a way of communicating a psychic state in which nothing can be known.

The specific use of −K that I discuss involves not knowing as a means of safeguarding one's very existence. When an individual's continuity of being is at stake, the individual is operating in a mode so fraught with panic that the individual is unable to make use of other people (for example, by means of healthy projective identification) to help the individual even temporarily to find safety through the use of the mind of another (who is not in a state of panic).

Bion (1962, 1970, 1992) contends that the drive to get to know (K) what is true to one's emotional experience is as important as the need for water or the need for sex. A person may live without sex but not without truth because without a way of sensing what is true, life has no meaning (Schneider, 2003). It seems to me that −K is a necessary partner to K, and that K and −K maintain an essential dynamic relationship with each other.[2]

DOI:10.4324/9781003384601-6

−K is not simply the absence of K – it is a purposeful attack on K, often motivated by an effort to avoid losing one's mind or one's sense of self. As human beings, we cannot tolerate knowing all of what is true to our emotional experience. At birth, the infant's separateness from the mother is too much for him or her to bear; that truth is held in safekeeping by the mother until the child's psychological capacity catches up with his or her physical reality of separateness. As Freud states in *Beyond the Pleasure Principle*, it is "almost more important" (1920/1955, p. 27) not to perceive as it is to perceive external reality. Freud, in this way, suggests that evasion of reality is essential for maintaining one's capacity to use one's mind to process incoming stimuli. He termed the mental function responsible for this filtering of percepts "the stimulus barrier" (p. 27). I have found Freud's concept of the stimulus barrier to be critical to my understanding of −K. Not perceiving is not simply a failure to perceive; it constitutes a psychic function in its own right; the safeguarding of sanity from breakdown as a consequence of being flooded by more external reality that one is able to psychologically process.

What Did Oedipus Know and Not Know?

I will now turn to a brief discussion of the central psychoanalytic myth, the myth of Oedipus, in which I delineate several levels and forms of attempts not to know. In doing so, I hope to demonstrate the centrality to psychoanalysis of the K/−K interplay.

The myth of Oedipus depicts Oedipus unknowingly killing Laius, his father, and marrying Jocasta, his mother. In Sophocles's version of the myth, Laius is told by the Oracle at Delphi that he is to die at the hands of his son. In an effort to escape his fate, he and Jocasta give the infant Oedipus to a shepherd who is to kill Oedipus in the mountains. Because the shepherd cannot bring himself to kill Oedipus, the infant is raised as the child of the King and Queen of Corinth (who are unable to have a child of their own.) When Oedipus learns from another oracle that his fate is to kill his father and marry his mother, he attempts to avert this catastrophe by leaving the King and Queen who he believes to be his parents. But in an encounter on the road where three roads meet, Oedipus kills a man (Laius) and his four servants.

At the entrance to Thebes, Oedipus solves the riddle of the Sphinx, who is holding Thebes in a state of siege. Oedipus's mental feat and act of courage lead to his becoming King of Thebes and marrying the widowed Queen of Thebes, Jacosta.

After Thebes suffers many years of famine as a consequence of the anger of the gods, Oedipus asks the blind seer, Tiresias, to tell him the source of the gods' anger. When Tiresias tries to tell Oedipus the truth – that Oedipus has killed his father and married his mother – Oedipus becomes enraged and refuses to hear the truth. Ultimately, Oedipus is unable to ignore the truth with which he is confronted, and realizes that he is the killer of his father, and the son of his wife, and "the unholy polluter of the land . . . living in shameful intercourse with his nearest of kin" (Watling, 1947).

Steiner writes that the "heroic moment" (1993, p. 119) when Oedipus faces the truth is the climax of the play. "'Alas! All out! All know! No more concealment! Oh light! May I never look on you again, revealed as I am, sinful in my begetting, sinful in marriage, sinful in shedding blood'" (Sophocles, quoted by Steiner, 1993, p. 122). Facing the truth, Jocasta hangs herself, and Oedipus blinds himself. Rather than seeing Oedipus as an innocent, however, Steiner suggests that Oedipus knew or "half-knew" the truth and so did those who surrounded him.

> It seems to me less certain that he fully knew all these facts, and it is more plausible that he half-knew them, and decided to turn a blind eye to this half-knowledge . . . Indeed, they dealt with unwelcome reality by *turning a blind eye.*
>
> Mechanisms such as *turning a blind eye*, which keep facts conveniently out of sight and allow someone to know and not to know, simultaneously, can be highly pathological and lead to distortions and misrepresentations of the truth. But it is important to recognize that *they still reflect a respect and a fear of the truth*, and it is this fear which leads to the collusion and the cover-up.
>
> (Steiner, 1993, p. 129, italics added)

The irony is that by not knowing throughout his life, there was in the end a catastrophe.

Oedipus desperately did not want fully to know the already half-known truth and attempted in his own mind as well as in his behavior to disregard and reject the truth for fear of recognizing that the prophesized catastrophe was inescapable or had already occurred. It is ironic that it was Oedipus's use of his mind in solving the riddle of the Sphinx that resulted in his becoming King of Thebes and marrying the Queen, his other.

Thus at its core, the central myth of psychoanalysis is a narrative depicting the psychological pain of a man who cannot bear to know the truth, not because he is cowardly but because he is human. Who could bear the weight of the knowledge that he will murder (or already has murdered) his father and will engage in incest with his mother? In the Oedipus myth, not knowing was not Oedipus's undoing – whether or not he knew the truth, the patricide and incest would occur. Not knowing was a humanly understandable way for Oedipus to attempt to live a life, a humanly tragic life. We are all destined to psychically kill our parents in the act of growing up (Loewald, 1979) and to harbor incestuous wishes. Fortunately, we are usually able not to know about such horrifying truths until we are sufficiently mature (as children or adults) and helped by our parents (or perhaps an analyst) to live with and make peace with these human truths (along with other almost unbearable truths, such as the inescapability of our own death). Not knowing is, indeed, almost more important than knowing.

I

Clinical Illustration

Ms. N called to set up an appointment with me and stated unequivocally that she "wanted to go into psychoanalysis." I sensed from her confident tone that she was a person familiar with psychoanalysis who knew what she wanted, perhaps someone from the analytic community. Yet I found myself wondering about her asking specifically for psychoanalysis. How could she be so sure what, if any, psychotherapeutic intervention she wanted from me, since she had not yet met me? These thoughts were of an unfocused sort.

Ms. N arrived promptly for our meeting. When I encountered her in the waiting room, I was struck by the contrast between my impressions of her confident stance on the phone and her appearance. She was a woman in her early thirties, pale, thin and somewhat waiflike, wearing mismatched and unkempt clothing.

Once Ms. N was seated in my consulting room, she began by telling me that she had "suppressed thinking about analysis for several years." She wanted to be in treatment because she was concerned that she was unable to stay in an "intimate relationship" for longer than a year and because she was "so tense" that she could not function fully at work due to pain in her back, hip, and knee. Ms. N told me that often she was barely able to get out of bed or muster the energy to walk from her bed to the bathroom to brush her teeth. She spoke in halting, incomplete sentences, punctuated by sighs and sounds of exasperation as if she were waiting for me to fill in the gaps for her (while being simultaneously fearful that I would).

After a brief pause, Ms. N recounted a dream that she had dreamed the previous night.

> I was falling apart and unable to support myself because I was fully incompetent, I was crazy. This is interesting because I have a life-long fear and recurring dream of becoming a bag lady – ending up on the street – losing everything. In the dream, I'm in a house with a roommate, and there are monsters outside – people deformed from a disease. There's a sense of evil – a sense of the *Night of the Living Dead*. Zombies are trying to get into the house – banging on the windows, they want in. I know I'm going to have to talk to them. They want some sort of payment. A young boy I know talks to me, saying, "Remember I told you I wasn't infected." Then he gets a scratch. I said, "Okay, we'll do something about it." As I take him over, he dies.

I was surprised at how easily Ms. N interjected the dream into our conversation, without a discernible change in tone or facial expression. I was to learn in subsequent meetings that it was characteristic of her to speak with this fluid mix of dream and reality, without a hint of hesitation or discomfort.

As Ms. N told me the dream, I noticed that she was physically tightening her whole body – her lips barely moved as she talked. Her eyes remained directed at me, but it seemed that she was no longer seeing me in a focused way. I said to her, "Something seems to be happening as you're talking with me. It's as if something has changed between the time of our phone conversation and our meeting in the waiting room." (It occurred to me that perhaps she had been as surprised in seeing me as I had been in seeing her.) She responded by looking away from me and saying, "My chest gets really tight; talking about this simply makes me feel like crying." She said that her thoughts had become confused – "mixing real and unreal." She did not know "which was which." "I have trouble keeping straight what is a dream, what is a memory, and what is something that is happening now."

When Ms. N stopped seeing me in a focused way and later looked away, it seemed that she could not tolerate being with me. Perhaps she was protecting me from her direct gaze, fearing that she would "take me over" as she had taken over the boy in the dream; that is, that she would take me into her psychosis – her state of mind in which dream and external reality are poorly differentiated. Such an outcome would mean the end of both of us as separate people.

After thinking for a moment, I said to her,

A: You seemed surprised by me. It's as if the simple act of meeting me has shaken your sense not only of who I am but also of who you are.

[I had a growing feeling that, perhaps, coexisting with her psychosis was a false-self or dissociated aspect of her personality.]

P: Funny . . . sounds right, and I found myself relaxing in hearing you say that, yet voices in me are saying, "No, don't relax." I don't let anyone know what I'm feeling, but that's good, it leads to the problem I had with my former therapist.

I felt confused and did not know what "it" referred to, what was "good," or what "problem" there had been.

P: J [I assumed that J was the name of the therapist] seldom asked questions or shed light on anything. I guess I want to come to analysis not just to find out why I'm unhappy – I could come up with logical explanations for that – but I want to get beyond the logical.

There was a marked change in her facial expression as she spoke. She looked stunned at her response, as if she could not believe what she had said. She seemed almost to be shrinking away in her chair. Her stated wish to get beyond the logical was so disconnected from and contradictory to her fear of going completely crazy that it felt strangely incongruous to me (and, I presume, to her).

Ms. N went on to tell me that her previous four attempts at psychotherapy had all been failures. In each case, she felt somehow responsible for the end of therapy, although, in telling me about these experiences, she spoke only of what the therapist had done or had failed to do. Ms. N described how, after an angry outburst, she was "kicked out" by one of her therapists who said, "There will be no anger in my office." Another therapist ended the work after Ms. N reported "a dream of abortion," to which he responded, "Don't be abusive with me." Still another therapist "threw a magazine at me with an article on anti-depressants and said, 'Unless you are lying about your symptoms, you should be on anti-depressants, not in therapy.'"

After hearing Ms. N's accounts of her previous experiences in psychotherapy, it seemed to me likely that she was blinding herself to the possibility that she and each of her previous therapists had been terrified of her underlying psychosis. Her therapist's "not allowing anger" seemed to me to be an only slightly disguised statement that the therapist could not tolerate Ms. N's psychosis or the way that she was engendering in the therapist a feeling that he was becoming psychotic. I saw the therapists (as described by the patient) as internal objects among who insanity was both contagious (some of which I felt in my own confusion) and steadfastly unacknowledged.

II

Ms. N, a 31-year-old administrator, was the youngest of four children; her next older sibling, a brother, was 10 years her senior. The patient told me that she was an "unwanted baby": "my mother had me in order to keep my father" (who was planning divorce once the other children were grown). Her father was furious when he learned of the pregnancy and ordered the mother to abort the fetus and have a post-natal hysterectomy.

I had the impression on hearing this that even before Ms. N's birth, there was no psychological space for her in the mind of either parent; and, perhaps, this underlay the denial that saturated her unconscious internal-object relationships. It seemed to me that her being adamant on the phone about wanting four-times-per-week analysis represented an unconscious effort to ensure herself a place with me (by presenting herself as an imaginary patient, the patient she believed I wanted her to be.)

In one of our first sessions, Ms. N told me several dreams. In one of them, "I was at a bookstore being chased by police (who were friends of mine) for stealing four books that I did not know I had stolen." She stopped there and said in a voice bordering on anger, "Nothing, there's nothing more to say!" Her abrupt shift shook me out of my usual way of listening (that is, a state of reverie in which I drift between the patient's words and my own unfocused thoughts). I somewhat reflexively suggested that this dream reflected a concern on her part that she could do harm to me and the analysis without intending to do so, perhaps by stealing my mind/books or by usurping my role as analyst. Only in retrospect was I aware that my intervention ignored the patient's angry outburst and my having been startled by it. After waiting for what seemed a long time, Ms. N commented, "Everything is slipping away. When I talk about my ideas, I lose them." Again in retrospect, the patient was telling me that she felt that she was losing me and her own mind.

Almost without pausing, she launched into another dream: "A glass table in a store with 40 delicate coffee pots on a table. A customer being reckless and knocked the table, causing a few of the pots to fall off the table and shatter. But I don't have any associations. I never trust my first impressions – they get foggy – it's not a good idea to trust anyone."

I said to her that the dream seemed to express her worry that the analysis would become reckless, out of control. How well would I be able to run a "store" that contained so many fragile things? It seemed to me that she was afraid that her thoughts would break the container of the analysis, that is, my ability to think and conduct myself as an analyst.

Both the dream of stealing four books and the dream of coffee pots shattering seemed to repeat the patient's anxiety about starting the analysis (which was to have a frequency of four sessions per week). At the same time, there was a glimmer of hopefulness to the dreams – not only were the police her friends, but also only some of the containers had broken, leaving more to withstand the jolts of her internal (and projected) chaos and her destructiveness.

As Ms. N was telling me the dream about the 40 pots, I was becoming extremely uneasy and anxious. Several stories came to mind: the story of Jesus spending 40 days in the desert fasting while being tempted by Satan; the story of Noah's ark where it rained for 40 days and 40 nights as punishment for man's greed and corruption; and the story of Ali Baba and the 40 thieves in the *Arabian Nights*. In this story, Ali Baba's greedy brother, Kasim, ends up butchered and cut into pieces by the 40 thieves for stealing "booty" that they themselves had stolen from the wealthy.

On the basis of these reveries, I said to the patient that I thought she was afraid that her demands on me were manifestations of her thievery, deceit, and greed for which she would be punished (perhaps by being broken, dismembered, or butchered). In addition, I would be damaged by her and unable or unwilling to work with her.

After saying this to Ms. N, I had a hollow sense that I was increasingly filling in the blanks with my "reveries," which I was taking literally and using rather mechanically in the absence of Ms. N's associations. I had known (half-known) for some time that, after I said something, Ms. N would quite often act as if the event or statement to which I was referring had never happened, thereby "blotting it out" and leaving me confused. For instance, Ms. N said, in response to a comment I made, "We already talked about this yesterday. I resent the hell out of it that what I say is not important enough for you to remember."

In the absence of Ms. N's ability to use her mind, I was substituting my mind for hers (using my reveries as if they were the patient's unconscious thoughts), while blinding myself to that fact. In so doing, I was protecting myself from the feeling that I, too, was utterly confused about what was really happening.

As I thought more about my defensive interventions, Ms. N told me another dream: "Something had lodged between one of my teeth and a gold crown. As I tried to dig it out with a toothpick, the tooth kept cracking deeper and deeper and seemed to have no bottom. Tried to get the food out, kept digging and digging, deeper and deeper. Never got it. No end." I noticed that just as the subject of her sentences disappeared as she told the dream – "tried to," "never got it," "no end" – the patient was disappearing as a separate subject as she gave in to her increasingly disowned desire that no longer felt like hers. Once again Ms. N had no associations to the dreams.

During the silence that followed her telling me the dream, I felt no need to provide the patient with associations of my own. In that period of silence, I became more fully aware of the extent to which I had been using my own reveries and associations to the patient's dreams not to enter into conscious and unconscious conversation with the patient but to obscure for myself my intolerance of not knowing what was happening and my anxiety about taking such a disturbed patient into analysis.

III

Ms. N and I continued exploring her request for psychoanalysis during the next several sessions. During this period, she warned me that she gets very depressed and sometimes feels like ending her life, but that she could tolerate these feelings if I could. There was a quality of self-awareness in this statement that I had not heard from her to this point. She said she hoped she would not frighten me off in the way she had alienated her previous therapists. We agreed on a schedule of four sessions per week and the use of the couch.

The work seemed to be going well for the first few months of analysis, but about 5 months into things, Ms. N began to forget meetings and would come on the wrong day or at the wrong time, and twice forgot to pay me. After my planned vacation break, she forgot the date we were to resume. In addition, she frequently forgot her keys or left her handbag in the consulting room or in the waiting room. In response to the patient's leaving these things, I suggested to her that she might have been leaving parts of herself for me to look after when she was not with me, fearing that she would be lost to me and to herself. Her wish to have a place in me and with me seemed connected to a fear of losing parts of herself.

Ms. N responded by saying,

P: When I was potty training, my mother gave me a piece of candy every time I used the toilet. She said the candy came from a bird. One day when we were walking in the park, we saw a dead bird and my mother said, "That's the bird that brought the candy. There will be no more candy." I stayed at the park all day next to the bird and cried.

A: You must have felt very frightened by the idea that all that was good, both within and outside of you, could be destroyed in an instant. There was no truly secure place or reliably loving person in the world for you, and there still isn't.

In this interchange, Ms. N was telling me that she had lost her mind as a consequence of her mother's cruelly shattering the symbol – more accurately, a "symbolic equation" (Segal, 1957) – of a loving connection with her mother, both as an internal and an external object. This "attack on linking" (Bion, 1959) is a manifestation of an attack on K, that is, an attack on all that the patient as a child thought she knew. The patient's subsequent use of not knowing as a way to defend herself against the pain of facing the truth of her mother's cruel attack is a manifestation of −K.

IV

Toward the end of the sixth month of analysis, I met Ms. N in the waiting room where she appeared noticeably agitated. In the previous session, the patient had talked about her mixing up numbers in street addresses and phone numbers despite the fact that she could do a very good job of keeping track of complicated numerical calculations in her work as a graphic designer. I had said to her in response that she had developed a way to keep part of her mind working well while another part felt unable to hold on to the facts that make up the reality of the world.

Once in the consulting room, she began by saying, "I've been having vivid dreams, night-time dreams, and also dreams during the day." She went on to tell me the following dream:

> I was in a forest with my brother and with men who were hunters and outlaws, and a man who looked like everyone else rode up on a white horse and shot at me while I tried to dart and crawl away. My brother killed the man with an axe and dismembered him. It was bloody and gory, but I wasn't horrified, just worried my brother would go crazy. To prevent himself from killing someone else, he cut off his arms and legs and reduced himself to an egg – lying in a pan – the doctor stirs the egg with his hands and my brother takes form.
>
> I woke up with the sense of disappearing, evaporating into the atmosphere. I know how that man could relate to you – he came from a place where everybody is the same, and I had fears of analysis bringing me into conformity – a beaten egg is also homogenized.

That Ms. N told me the dream reflected the fact that she trusted me with primitive and psychotic aspects of herself – something she had feared doing, beginning with our initial phone conversation. Speaking to her about my perceptions, I said,

A: The idea of continuing with me in analysis feels like a very dangerous thing for you to do, and yet you've taken that risk. I think that you hope that the dreams will show me – not just tell me – something about who you are that you've been afraid would frighten me off. I think you experience yourself as being as grotesque and horrifying as the figures in the dream. Even the doctor in the dream gets pulled into the horror as he mixes with his hands the remains of the body of a person who has amputated his limbs in order not to murder anyone else. I take quite literally your fear that you could crack up and take me down with you. But at the same time, I know that you are also showing me, in telling me the dream, that you're willing to take that risk on the basis of what you've experienced with me to this point.

P: [in a subdued voice] Yes, that's right. But I don't know what to do with it – the pain.

After a long pause, she told me another dream.

P: I was traveling on an expedition in the Sahara Desert. Something was wrong; mine was the only tent. I stepped out of the tent at sunset for a walk. As I walked further and further, it got darker and darker, and the wind picked up and was blowing sand everywhere and erasing my footprints. I had no idea which way to go back to the tent. All I remember is touching my face and being surprised that it felt like sand and not skin. In an odd way, there was something pleasant about the dream.

I felt for a moment that Ms. N had understood something of what I was attempting to convey in my interventions – a sense that she was disappearing – but that she was not yet able to make full use of this in her conscious thinking. She could only respond with an expression of pain and the telling of some dreams.

V

Ms. N left me a message canceling our next session because of an unexpected "conflict" around her work schedule that required she be out of town. She began the subsequent meeting by immediately saying,

> I've noticed over the last couple of days that I've stopped dreaming, or I've had dreams and can't recall them, and I've had these weird symptoms – a backache, and headaches, and I've been tense, stiff, and achy all over. I was thinking today that since the last time I saw you, I have filled up all my time – made more commitments than I can meet.

She went on to say (as if it were no different from her report of her aches and pains),

> Oh, something happened yesterday – or was it the day before – that unnerved me. I called to cancel an appointment with Dr. B because I forgot who you were and thought Dr. B was you. [Dr. B was an analyst with whom Ms. N had met for a consultation appointment before she consulted with me. She had canceled her subsequent appointment with Dr. B after having met with me.] I had Dr. B's phone number on my desk calendar from many months ago when I met with him before I saw you. I called his office and then his home. I felt utterly confused. I had no idea who he was or why I was calling him. He was also confused. He said, "I thought you canceled months ago," and I said, "I'm sorry. I thought you canceled months ago." I was completely flustered. I could only repeat his words.

Initially I was left speechless by what Ms. N had told me. Perhaps this was yet another way she rendered impotent my capacity to think. I then wondered (silently) if Ms. N's disorganized behavior, canceled meeting, and confusing Dr. B and me were related to the very disorganized and disintegrative dream that she had reported before missing her recent session. In the session before the one she canceled, she had given me the impression that she had been able to make some use of my interpretation concerning her fear of pulling me into her psychosis, alongside her feeling that I was strong enough to withstand the pull. I was taken by surprise by the fact that she had not only obliterated my interpretation, but she had obliterated me and a large part of herself in what seemed to be a negative hallucination (Green, 1975).[3] Both she and I had been "erased like footprints in the sand."

I felt that it was important for me to communicate as best I could my understanding of what it was that she was trying to tell me about what was happening to her.[4] I told Ms. N,

A: I think you're showing me in these different ways – forgetting you ever met me, forgetting our sessions ever occurred, forgetting what happened in the last session, not knowing who you are or why you're doing what you're doing – that you are capable of amputating your mind, just as the figure in the dream amputated his arms and legs. I think you're no longer willing to continue to hide from me or from yourself the terrifying experience of losing your mind and losing yourself. [I later added] In a way, I think that what I said in our last session led you to feel freer to experience what it feels like to lose your mind, since you feel some confidence that I can help you survive it without being killed or driven crazy myself.

P: What you say has been true for a long time. I have a problem with my mother because she won't remember certain things.

I was aware that she was only able to speak about what was happening between us for a few seconds before displacing her feelings about me on to her mother.

P: She doesn't remember the last 3 of the years we lived together. She doesn't remember hitting me. She doesn't remember going to counseling with me, even though we were in the same office. Two years after I moved out, I came back and visited her for the first time from college. I arrived in the evening as planned, and I had to break into the house because she forgot I was coming home. She has written me out of her life. She says I have never been in her life.

Ms. N was saying something in passing, and I was hearing the significance of it that she was not able to hear because of her fear of knowing.

A: I want to repeat something you just said – you haven't ever been in her life.

Through my shift in tone and change in cadence while repeating her words, I was emphasizing what she knew but could not yet fully think (that is, could not fully utilize in doing psychological work). I was repeating her words simply to frame them. Later I said, "Your mother has become not only part of what you think about, but also a part of the way you think – thinking with holes in which you lose who you are and who I am."

Discussion

My work with Ms. N began during our initial phone conversation, in which she was "unequivocal" (of one voice, one perspective) in her request for psychoanalysis. This engendered in me a (falsely knowing) reverie that she was a candidate for psychoanalysis, and probably part of the psychoanalytic community. When we met one another in the waiting room, we were both surprised.

This early shared experience of surprise led me to reconsider my first impression of her and to speak to her in a way that was respectful of her defensive need "not to know" herself or what she was doing with me. I saw her request for psychoanalysis as an expression of −K, a request for what appeared to be a deep analytic involvement while revealing as little as possible to me about her self. Ms. N seemed to fear an as-yet-unknown catastrophe – a catastrophe involving her being "introduced to herself."

"So few people think it is important to be introduced to themselves, but the one partner the patient can never get rid of while that patient is alive is himself" (Bion, 1980, p. 12).

The dream about the 40 pots led to a series of reveries on my part, including ones about Jesus in the desert, Noah's ark, and Ali Baba. I used these reveries as the basis for a set of interventions. I became aware that I had come to take my "reveries" (as I did in our initial phone conversation) as "clinical facts" (Britton & Steiner, 1994) and was defensively treating my formulations as "overvalued ideas" (p. 1070), perhaps because of my inability to contain my uncertainty. By taking my reveries so literally and offering interpretations derived from them, I was attempting to protect myself from my own state of confusion and from recognizing the depth of Ms. N's pathology.

While the manifest content of Ms. N's dreams involved many images of greed, I did not experience her as greedy; rather, I saw her as frightened of the effects she felt she would have on me and on the analysis. She seemed to experience her ordinary needs as greed. This transformation of need into greed served to help her not to know or accept her ordinary human needs. She resorted to an attack on her capacity to think, to know, or to feel anything for fear of experiencing herself as destructive to me (in the maternal transference) by needing me. To destroy me/her mother as a consequence of her greed would be equivalent to losing her mind and her self.[5]

After working with Ms. N for several months, I became increasingly aware that things were regularly not as they seemed, including her apparent engagement in, and feelings of, relief derived from our work. I eventually came to understand that the patient's seemingly enthusiastic reactions to my interpretations and her compliance represented forms of −K (self-protective pseudo-understanding), in that she was not actually making psychological use of what she and I were saying to one another.

Ms. N felt that she had to steal the analysis from me (as in her dream of unknowingly stealing books) because she feared that she would overwhelm me, harm me, and destroy the analysis if I (or she) came to know too much of who she is. Ms. N's fear that she would have to steal the analysis from me by concealing her insanity and destructiveness was key to my coming to understand that her imitation and undermining of genuine thinking and feeling (which I view as forms of −K) represented manifestations of her need to safeguard what remained of her very being. For Ms. N, to know was equivalent to being overwhelmed by the fear of her destructiveness; not to know was to be able to remain sane (albeit in a fragile state).

My interpretations of her dream of dismemberment seemed to have been of value to her while she was in my consulting room. But soon after leaving my office, she dismantled what she had come to know about her sense of impending loss of her mind by not only evacuating the thought but also by attacking her capacity for thinking and remembering.

I viewed her negative hallucination as an extreme form of −K. Instead of psychotically constructing a delusion as a reflection of her internal world, an entire sector of experience was obliterated. It was an annihilation of me as well as her capacity for thinking and remembering – a destruction of K. Paradoxically, the negative hallucination was a first step toward K in that it reflected an unconscious willingness to fully experience her psychosis in the context of her relationship with me, and to communicate that psychotic process to me.

I, too, began to better tolerate not knowing in the form of experiencing my own doubts ("negative capability") and confusions as potentially fertile states. I spoke to Ms. N about her experience in a way I hoped would not overwhelm her need not to know, while at the same time introducing something new to her, if only by means of the tone of my voice. By repeating her sentence almost word for word – "You haven't ever been in her life" – I was attempting to maintain a balance between respecting her defensive need not to know and offering something just new enough that she might be able to make use of it psychologically. Ogden refers to this form of intervention as an effort "to underscore the ways in which the patient knew, but did not know that he knew" (2003, p. 603).

In sum, my focus in this chapter has been on the survival value of not knowing (−K). I have proposed a use of −K that is not principally driven by envy but by the attempt to survive. There is an adaptive function of misunderstanding that serves to communicate one's intolerance of getting to know what is true to one's experience. Such forms of not knowing or not wanting to know represent ways of protecting oneself against the catastrophe of the destruction of one's mind as a consequence of knowing what one is not prepared to know (either as a child or as an adult).

Notes

1   Bion used the word "thinking" to include both thinking and feeling.
2   It must be borne in mind throughout this discussion that, despite the similarity of language, the concept of "negative capability" – "a tolerance of uncertainty, mysteries, and doubts" (Keats, quoted by Bion, 1962, p. 89) – and the concept of −K address diametrically opposite phenomena. Negative capability is a quality of K. −K is intolerance of doubt; it is an active, decisive mis-knowing and misunderstanding.
3   A negative hallucination is a transformation in −K: the projection of a psychic void onto an aspect of unbearable external reality.
4   Bion (1967) suggests that, under circumstances where the patient seems not to be able to think, we speak to the non-psychotic part of the personality about the psychotic part of the personality. It is with this in mind that I spoke to Ms. N about her negative hallucinosis, a manifestation of −K. I took the patient's negative hallucination not simply as a breakdown of K but as a communication of the experience of −K.
5   This is an example of −K in the form of moralistic misunderstandings, a concept Bion wrote about extensively but did not explicitly tie to −K.

References

Bion, W. R. (1959). Attacks on linking. *International Journal of Psychoanalysis, 40*, 308–315.
Bion, W. R. (1962). *Learning from experience*. Basic Books.
Bion, W. R. (1965). Transformations. In *Seven servants*. Jason Aronson.
Bion, W. R. (1967). *Second thoughts: Selected papers on psychoanalysis*. Jason Aronson.
Bion, W. R. (1970). *Attention and interpretation*. Tavistock Publications.
Bion, W. R. (1980). *Bion in New York and Sao Paulo* (F. Bion, Ed.). Clunie.
Bion, W. R. (1992). *Cognitions* (F. Bion, Ed.). Karnac Books.

Britton, R., & Steiner, J. (1994). Interpretation: Selected fact or overvalued idea? *International Journal of Psychoanalysis, 75*, 1069–1078.

Freud, S. (1955). Beyond the pleasure principle. In J. Strachey (Ed. & Trans.), *Standard edition of the complete psychological works of Sigmund Freud* (Vol. 18, pp. 7–64). Hogarth Press. (Original work published 1920)

Green, A. (1975). The analyst, symbolization, and absence in the analytic setting. In *On private madness*. International University Press.

Grotstein, J. S. (2004). The light militia of the lower sky: The deeper nature of dreaming and phantasying? *Psychoanalytic Dialogue, 14*, 99–118.

Loewald, H. (1979). The waning of the Oedipus complex. In *Papers on psychoanalysis*. Yale University Press.

Ogden, T. (2003). What's true and whose idea was it? *International Journal of Psychoanalysis, 84*, 593–606; *86*, 1–20.

Schneider, J. A. (2003). Janus-faced resilience in a severely traumatized patient. *Psychoanalytic Review, 90*, 869–887.

Schneider, J. A. (2005). Dreaming the truth of experience: Film note on "Heaven." *Psychoanalytic Review, 92*(5), 777–785.

Segal, H. (1957). Notes on symbol formation. *International Journal of Psychoanalysis, 38*, 391–397.

Steiner, J. (1993). *Psychic retreats*. Routledge.

Watling, E. F. (1947). *The Theban plays*. Penguin Books.

Janus-Faced Resilience in the Analysis of a Severely Traumatized Patient

"Was mich nicht umbringt, macht mich starker."[1]
– Friedrich Wilhelm Nietzsche, *Twilight of the Idols*, 1889

Resilience is something we ask of ourselves every day – and the rapidity of change and ferociousness of the world demands it of us. In today's world, we seem continually to be asked to adjust, and we attempt to do so without losing too much of ourselves. That necessary – even life- or sanity-preserving – resilience is a way of responding to disjunctions in life while attempting to maintain the continuity of who we are even as we are being changed by experience. But we can never be certain where the line lies between, on the one hand, healthy acts of giving up something of who we are in deference to the needs of others, and on the other hand, sacrificing so much of who we are that we cease being and becoming ourselves.

My principal intent in the case that follows is to describe what may be a universal phenomenon relating to the price we pay for being resilient. No clinical experience has so clarified for me the complex linkages among trauma, resilience, and symbolization as my work with this severely traumatized patient. The destructive effects of trauma on psychical organization have been well documented in the analytic literature; in contrast, little mention has been made of the psychological cost of resilience.

In this chapter, I discuss an analytic experience that involved efforts on the part of both the patient and myself to understand the patient's individual form of resilience and to use that understanding to facilitate emotional growth. The unfolding analytic experience was often a surprising – and humbling – endeavor. I came to understand on the basis of my experience in the analytic relationship both the healthy aspect of resilience that sustained the patient through her extensive traumatic experiences, as well as the pathological underbelly of her resilience – her intense conscious and unconscious anxiety regarding the damages inherent in emotional connections with others; the possibility of losing her capacity for absolute self-reliance; and the dangers posed by any interference with her ability to take immediate actions as a way of dealing with both real and imagined events.

DOI:10.4324/9781003384601-7

Theoretical Underpinnings

Freud (1915/1957, 1920/1955, 1926/1959) used an economic metaphor to characterize trauma as helplessness in the face of growing tension resulting from "an accumulation of amounts of stimulation" which cannot be discharged (1926/1959, p. 137). He understood trauma as the influx (from within or from the outside) of excessive quantities of excitation that overwhelm the psyche. According to Freud, the overtaxing stimulation caused by the sheer quantity of incoming excitation is too powerful to be managed and thus leads to permanent psychic disturbance.[2]

Further understanding of trauma can be gleaned from Bion's work. Although Bion (1962) never addressed trauma directly, in elaborating his theory of functions, he introduced several terms – "alpha elements," "beta elements," and "alpha function" – which are useful in considering the concept of trauma. These concepts afford greater understanding of how conscious and unconscious experiences are organized and given meaning, and how experience can be denuded of meaning.

In Bion's (1962) conceptualization, beta elements are raw sensory impressions that are un-utilizable for making linkages in the process of creating meaning. Thus they are suitable only for evacuation; for example, in hallucinations, perversions, and expulsive actions such as treatment-destructive acting-in or acting-out.

Alpha function is Bion's (1962) theoretical construct referring to a set of mental operations through which meaning is attributed to experience (the transformation of beta elements into alpha elements). Alpha elements can be linked in the process of creating personal meanings, which meanings can be stored as memory. Alpha function is necessary for dreaming and thinking during both waking and sleeping life.

Optimally, alpha function transforms raw sensory data (beta elements) first into perceptions linked with feeling and then into symbols, thereby making them available for fantasizing and dreaming and other forms of conscious and unconscious psychological work. Without the capacity to transform beta elements into alpha elements, a person is unable to generate differentiable conscious and unconscious experience, and can no longer distinguish between being awake and being asleep, or between dreaming and perceiving (Bion, 1970; Grotstein, 2000, 2002; Ogden, 2001, 2003). Without alpha function, the individual "cannot go to sleep and cannot wake up" (Bion, 1962, p. 7).

Alpha function and dreaming are overlapping processes by which a person generates and modifies emotional experience. If alpha function is defective, psychical processes stagnate; one can neither generate thoughts with which to do psychological work, nor learn from experience in both the external and internal object world. Under such circumstances, a person's capacities for thinking and creating do not evolve; when linkages cannot be made, elements of experience do not add up to anything.

As I am conceiving of it, trauma overwhelms alpha function. The over-stimulation that is definitive of trauma produces an excess of beta elements that "spill over the top," unable to be transformed by paralyzed, over-stretched alpha function into alpha elements. Consequently, all psychic energies are used in the service of keeping raw beta elements at bay: "Beta elements are dealt with [in the absence or paralysis of alpha function] by an evacuating procedure similar to the movements of musculature" (Bion, 1962, p. 13).[3]

Dreaming is central to Bion's (1962) conception of what it means to be alive as a human being. In Bion's terms, analysis allows conscious, lived experience in the outside world to be made available to dreaming (both unconscious waking dreaming and dreaming while asleep), and to make the unconscious available for conscious work, as in reverie and memory. In a genuine dream,[4] images and narratives are generated in the process of the dreamer's doing unconscious psychological work.

In cases of childhood psychic trauma, as important to the psychic development as the severity of the abuse or neglect may be the degree to which the child is alone with the experience. If an infant's mother is unable to live with, digest, and dream/create reveries of the infant's traumatic experience, the infant is left with "nameless dread" (Bion, 1967, p. 116) which is even more chaotic and stripped of meaning than the experience had been before the infant entrusted it to the mother. Of paramount importance is the mother's capacity to provide the infant a reverie state in which she may be able to "digest" the infant's projected, un-metabolized experience. Bion (1962), however, points out that:

> An infant endowed with marked capacity for tolerating frustration might survive the ordeal of a mother incapable of reverie and therefore incapable of supplying its needs. At the other extreme, an infant markedly incapable of tolerating frustration cannot survive without breakdown even [if he has] the experience of [healthy] projective identification with a mother capable of reverie; nothing less than unceasing breastfeeding would serve, and that is not possible through lack of appetite if for no other reason.
>
> (p. 37)

Without specifically taking up the issue of resilience, I believe Bion is suggesting here that, even in the absence of maternal reverie, an infant with marked capacity for tolerating frustration – the resilient infant – is able to compensate to some degree for a mother's inability to generate reverie states in which to create meaning from the infant's projected traumatic experience.

The theories of Freud and Bion share the underlying premise that psychic trauma involves excessive, intolerable emotional experience with which one is incapable of dealing. Freud would have it that this results in psychic upheaval and tireless efforts to cordon off the phenomena from conscious awareness, that is, by means of repression and symptom formation. Bion (1962) would add that the traumatized individual also attempts to rid the unconscious of emotional turbulence by shutting down the psychic function of generating conscious and unconscious meaning (i.e., alpha function).

I

Clinical Illustration

In the case that follows, I offer a detailed account of psychoanalytic work with Ms. A, a 33-year old professional dancer, who, in the face of repeated violent physical and psychological trauma beginning in childhood, was able to preserve significant aspects of her creative potential. The patient's ability to sustain such creative potential reflected one aspect of what I think of as the resilience of her personality.

In our initial telephone conversation, Ms. A spoke rapidly, jumping from topic to topic. She seemed to be a nightmare tenuously patched together – someone bursting at the seams. Listening to her, I had images of strained nuts, bolts, and rivets popping off – and fragmented objects held together with chewing gum.

Ms. A said she had been referred by a nutritionist for help with her eating disorder, and she wanted me to help her control her weight although she described herself as slim. I suspected the nutritionist had felt there was something problematic about someone already thin requesting a program that would help her to lose weight. After a few minutes of listening to Ms. A, I also suspected the nutritionist had felt overwhelmed by her.

Ms. A said she was told by several orthopedists that she would have to stop dancing because, despite multiple surgeries and an endless series of consultations, her left knee was failing. She said that she thought that if I could help her lose weight, she might salvage her knee, which would allow her to continue dancing. She said that without dance, she felt there was no reason to go on living.

There was a breathless urgency – almost desperation – in Ms. A's voice, so I asked if it was only her weight with which she wished help. In a tense voice, she said that she had been depressed for a long time, and recently her depression had worsened. She had been unable to leave her bed for days, and she was thinking about killing herself. She said she had considered using a gun to suicide, but had been cautioned by a physician that if the gun misfired, she might live, but in a fully incapacitated state.

She told me that her aunt, one of the few people she loved who was still alive, was hospitalized in critical condition after having been hit by a car the previous week. Her grandmother had recently died. And her father was in prison for the violent murder of her mother 3 years earlier.

I found myself speechless, not knowing whether to take literally what the patient had told me. I wondered if she would commit suicide even before we got off the phone. I felt caught off-guard and uncertain that I could offer what she seemed to be asking for. It seemed to me that what she was telling me – dramatic as the history seemed – was not the whole story concerning her reasons for seeking analysis.

I felt she was coming to analysis as a matter of survival, saying, in effect, "My life is in your hands." I tried to set these impressions aside as I worked to regain my composure. When she pleadingly asked me again if I could help her lose weight, I suggested that we needed to talk in person. I also said I thought she was asking if I would feel overwhelmed by her circumstances, as the nutritionist may have felt.

Ms. A let what I said about the need to meet in person hang for a moment as she considered this. She had called just before a holiday. Because of my vacation plans, I could not offer her a session until my return to the office several days later. We agreed she needed to see someone sooner, so I gave her the names of several colleagues, and we agreed that if need be, she could use the services of a hospital emergency room.

Although I was alarmed by the details of her story, as I listened to her, I also sensed an inner strength, perhaps my response to her ability to listen and consider what I was saying. In fact, the next day, she left a message saying that she had found our phone conversation helpful: she said that she felt understood by me and was able to think more clearly, and had decided to wait for an appointment with me. Her decision seemed to indicate she was able to step outside of herself and, for the time being, suspend her usual approach, which was to take action. I felt a sense of relief, but I continued to wonder what I could offer her, which reflected my own internal pressure to take action.

II

During our first encounter in the waiting room, I found Ms. A to be of short stature and somewhat boyish with cropped hair, black pants, T-shirt, black jacket, and thick-soled black oxford shoes.

Once seated in my office, she began by saying that after our phone conversation, she had used a TENS unit (an electrical device to relieve chronic pain), and because of it, her knee felt better. I was aware that she did not comment on our exchanges on the phone, and that instead, she focused on taking action for relief of physical (and psychical) pain. I experienced a fleeting background sensory image of a mechanical, machine-like apparatus that moved her knees and arms.[5] I said to her, "From what you said on the phone, being unable to dance scares you to death, and you feel you have nowhere to turn." I based my comment on what I intuited from the small bits of history she had given me and from her "knee-jerk" self-reliance, which was reflected in her attributing relief to the TENS unit which had no connection with me or any other human being. She was coming to analysis because her life depended on it. But she could not and would not depend on me.

Ms. A acknowledged my comment, and went right on to tell me a bit about her work as an assistant to a stockbroker. After her father was sent to prison, she took on the responsibility of managing their finances. "I trained to be a stockbroker to get the most out of the finances that I possibly could." [I viewed this as a form of operational resilience that served to avoid feelings of fear and isolation.]

At work, the patient constructed the veneer of a savvy assistant, which very effectively led co-workers not to suspect that the patient's life was full of pain, somatic illness, and unspeakable trauma. She went on to tell me that she had undergone numerous knee surgeries and currently was compulsively bingeing and vomiting, restricting her food intake, and using drugs and alcohol excessively (Schneider, 1990, 1995).

Ms. A told me how cruel her father had been to her mother and how helpless she had felt when she could not defend her. She also described her own fear of murdering someone (which she had felt from the time she was 8 years old). She told me in detail about her anger at men. I commented that I wondered if she was warning both of us that I was taking my life in my hands in seeing her. Her response to my interpretation was an unenthusiastic nod of agreement. My interpretation about her fear of her anger felt flat and predictable to me as well.

III

Ms. A began the next session by immediately telling me a dream that she had had the night before the session. "The dream took place in a house – in a cozy den with soft carpets on the floor, a fire flickering in the fireplace, and a dog resting on the floor next to a large comfortable easy chair."

The patient went on to say that the dream was pleasant, and the den was in the kind of house she had always dreamed of having. "When I was a child, I drew detailed drawings of a dream house. My father found them and angrily took them from me and said, 'Who do you think you are?' I stopped drawing after that."

My first impression was that the images in the dream represented the sense of hope Ms. A held that analysis would provide what had been missing from her childhood. As she continued speaking, I became aware that the "hope" came as much from me as from Ms. A's dream (which was devoid of people).

My mind wandered to Ernest Hemingway's *In Another Country*, a short story I had not thought about for many years. Set in Milan, the story is about several soldiers who returned from the front lines with physical and emotional scars. Daily they went to a physical rehabilitation center. There, each man sat in a new, mysterious, and untested mechanical apparatus while being instructed about its miraculous curative capabilities by a doctor whose fanatical enthusiasm was transparent to the reader. The knee of a major – who had once been the greatest fencer in Italy – was frozen in a boomerang-like position as a result of his wound, but he was told that, with the help of the machine, he would return to being a great fencer. The doctor displayed sets of before and after photographs on the wall as testimonials, while, in fact, these soldiers were the first ever to use the machine.

With this story in mind, I recalled my earlier sensory image of Ms. A's mechanical treatment of her non-responsive knee, her visits to numerous doctors' offices, and her use of a TENS unit to electronically stimulate her knee. I also recalled her comment that when her knee would not function as she demanded, she felt like "smashing it against the wall." At times she spoke to her knee in brutalizing tones as she tried to get more out of it than there was, using the language of a parent abusing a child: "Take that. You think this hurts. I'll show you what real pain is! Just you wait!" At the same time, I was all the more aware of the mechanical quality of my previous interpretations.

My response to the dream shifted at this point. I became aware that the dream had qualities that felt clichéd. I was also aware of the sharp contrast between the manifest dream content and the series of images that it elicited in me. This led me to view the dream setting as being too perfect, as if staged, like a glossy page from a Martha Stewart catalog. The dream was perhaps a manic attempt to fill in with hope the depths of despair and emptiness; an unconscious attempt to make something (me and the analysis) into more than it appeared to be; and to hold onto what she possibly could of a sense of self in the face of impending psychic fragmentation.

It seemed to me that if we were to continue in this way, we would not have an analysis but rather a safe and comfortable one-dimensional experience together as depicted in Ms. A's dream of "letting a sleeping dog lie." All of this took place within me in a matter of moments, and I decided not to respond further to the dream just then.

Ms. A began the next meeting by telling me that when she left my office after the previous meeting, she stopped at a nearby café and filled herself with food, then forced herself to vomit.

Apparently the "cozy" dream – like beautifully presented food gone bad – once taken in, could not sustain her and in fact was toxic. Her idealizing relationship with me, which she so rapidly gobbled up, was not digestible or sustainable. She could not hold in what she had made of me. For Ms. A, "taking me in" involved exaggerating what she had garnered from what had actually happened.

In the next few sessions, we agreed to work together at a slightly reduced fee 4 meetings per week with the patient using the couch.

IV

Ms. A described her mother as an alcoholic and manic-depressive who experienced multiple breakdowns with subsequent hospitalization and treatment with ECT therapy. It seemed that whenever the patient made a move toward independence, her mother suffered a breakdown (for example, when Ms. A graduated from grade school, performed in dance recitals, graduated from high school, and moved out of the house). Her mother's "breakdowns" included slitting her own wrists, "accidentally" setting her bed and herself on fire, and overdosing on drugs. On some of these occasions, Ms. A cancelled her planned activity and took her mother to the hospital. In listening to these accounts, I experienced an odd sense of confusion. Was I taking care of Ms. A (in offering to see her at a reduced fee), or was she taking care of my need to be an analyst (by agreeing to meet 4 times a week using the couch)?

Ms. A asked me, "Who will take care of me if I have a breakdown like my mother did?" Given her history, I could well understand Ms. A's fear that being in analysis might mean she was as crazy as her mother or might get even crazier than her mother to a point that she would never regain her sanity.

I said to her, "I think you're telling me that you may know more than I do – more than you'd like to – about what it's like to be responsible for someone who is so sick that you have no idea how to go about taking care of them."

Ms. A responded, "She was so out of control – so deaf and so addicted – hell-bent on destroying herself. There was no helping her. We were doing this little dance together, and there was no perspective because we were so close."

Following this meeting, Ms. A told me a dream, which consisted simply of the knowledge that her mother was dead. I felt the dream attempted an exorcism of her own felt state of demonic possession, an attempt to dis-identify with her mother whom she had kept alive inside her internal object world. Even after death, Ms. A had protected her mixed-up link with her mother, attempting to keep her alive by means of a near-psychotic identification with her (for example, in her tirade against her knee).

I said I thought she spent a good deal of her life trying to be sure she was not as crazy as her mother; but to loosen her grip on that idea was to lose touch with her mother, and to lose her mother is also to lose herself.

She responded, "I was afraid when I began seeing you that you were going to force me to see things through your eyes, but you haven't. I can take what I want and choose to disagree without feeling too much fear that you're going to tear into me." She went on to say, "This may seem odd, but just talking with you in this way is a relief. There are just the two of us here."

Ms. A's mother's final breakdown came when Ms. A moved to her own apartment. The following day, her father murdered her mother. During Ms. A's dance rehearsal, her uncle came to tell her that her mother was dead. Ms. A kept on dancing – "going about my business" – so as not to get caught up in the sickness of the family, but at the cost of splitting off the experience of loss or even of change. "After Mom died and Dad was in jail, I had to clean up the house and mop up the blood stains off the floor so the house could be sold."

Ms. A told me the following dream in a subsequent session. "I was eating slices of turkey with tomato, and someone asked me why I was not putting them inside slices of bread to make a sandwich." I said to her, "You seem to be saying to yourself and to me in the dream, 'If I have no bread, I can still make a sandwich and feed myself.'"

There was no doubt that Ms. A had impressive strengths with which to deal with her chaotic outer world, and that she had managed to do a great deal with the crumbs life in the external world had made available to her. In spite of all that was happening at home, Ms. A did well in school and eventually enrolled at a major university where she went on to receive a Master's in Fine Arts. Even though her parents had sufficient financial means, she did not want to rely on their grudging support, and so she decided not to ask them for money. In college and graduate school, she used food stamps and medical care at a city-operated medical clinic.

V

Not long after the meetings just discussed, Ms. A began a session (as she frequently did) by telling me a dream. "A little girl was in a room with a man. And I was watching. The little girl had bandages on her thighs. Her father put her in a cage with animals, birds. The birds started tearing at her, shredding her, especially her legs. She realized her fright was not from fear of the physical pain, but from the emotional pain of being thrown into the cage and being ripped apart."

She went on to say, "I was thinking about the very first time I talked to you on the phone. I was desperate; but it was amazing to have someone listen to me and not get frightened or angry even though what was happening was so overwhelming. I told you quite a bit about my life over the phone, which is very unusual for me."

Ms. A was silent for a moment. During this brief period of quiet, I found myself thinking about the contrast between this dream and the earlier dream depicting the perfect "dream house." It seemed to me that the patient in the current dream was both the one being thrown into the cage and the un-pictured one throwing her in. The patient's throwing herself into the cage with animals seemed in part to depict her conflicted wish to throw herself into analysis which she feared would involve the unleashing of primitive, inescapable, savage forces. She had previously thrown herself into the cage of her mother's insanity, which also seemed to me to be represented in the dream imagery.

During this and subsequent meetings Ms. A was able to allow herself to imagine or feel she was breaking down (feeling "shredded") while feeling held together by me during and after the meeting. This was a shift for her. Her resilient temperament, as seen in this dream as well as the dream of the cozy den, was to start with a view of herself as whole that she held sacred and kept impenetrable. But this kept her from looking at the deeper anxiety that felt like a threat to her survival.

VI

Over the course of the analysis, Ms. A told me more of what it had been like for her to live with her father. The patient described how she had lived in fear of retaliation from her father when she took care of her mother, particularly when she drove her mother home from the hospital after one or another of her mother's suicide attempts. On one occasion when she brought her mother home, her father locked them both outside. At another time, Mr. A threw water on her bed (symbolically urinating on it) to retaliate for Ms. A's having helped her mother. On such nights, Ms. A slept in the neighbor's car until her father left for work at 2:00 A.M., at which time she crawled through her bedroom window to get back into the house.

Mr. A could not stand any of Ms. A's attachments. He tortured her pets, and on one occasion, Ms. A arrived home to discover that her father, in a fit of rage, had "disposed" of her collie and bragged about it. She learned from such experiences to anticipate her father's actions, and when he talked about getting rid of subsequent dogs, Ms. A took pre-emptive action – in one instance finding a farmer who was willing to give her dog a home, in another, bringing the dog to the humane society rather than having her father kill it. While Ms. A's anticipating her father's behavior toward her dogs was no doubt a resourceful response at the time, it also contributed to the pathological consequences of her brand of resilience. Taking immediate decisive action undercut the patient's tolerance for living with feared dangers and being able to differentiate between real and imagined danger.

As Ms. A was telling me about her handling of her father, a story came to my mind which the patient had told me some months earlier about how she learned to swim: "Dad dunked me in the water. I had to learn to swim or drown, but it worked. I never had a fear of the water, and I became a good swimmer and was on the swim team." While Ms. A spoke of this with a sense of pride, it was evident that she had never taken pleasure in swimming; her defensive sense of accomplishment was disconnected from the grim inhumanity of the "sink or swim" mentality with which she was more strongly identified.

When Ms. A was 27, her father killed her mother with a fatal blow from his fist that smashed her spleen and broke her back. He was found guilty of manslaughter and sentenced to life in prison.

In the course of the subsequent year of analysis, Ms. A began to speak of her father as a man who was neither purely monstrous nor idealized. She recalled that when she was 5, her father taught her how to dance, carefully tracing her feet on cardboard, cutting out the cardboard imprints, and taping them on the floor in the proper position for the steps to the cha-cha-cha. He was her dance partner and called her "Princess" as they danced. When Ms. A was 10 years old, he bought her a set of drums. He played the clarinet and saxophone, while she accompanied him on the drums – making music together.

Her father had wanted a boy, so as a child, Ms. A got her hands on plumbing books and other home improvement manuals and helped her father around the house as a "tomboy." Astoundingly, Ms. A had found enough in her father as he actually was to be able to carve a relationship with him that was far more than a false-self relationship based on compliance. Put another way, Ms. A was able to create an internal place in which to hold onto healthy elements of the real relationship with her father.

VII

Ms. A decided that if she could not dance, at least she could make dances, so she began to choreograph and eventually had some of her dances performed on stage. She also began painting, and, to her surprise, found a particular form of pleasure in painting with colors, perhaps a reflection of the developing internal aliveness she was feeling.

She said, "In painting, as with dance, I have a space where I can suspend judgment and practical thinking. I can look at what I've painted and be surprised by it. I look at it to see "who I am." Ms. A seemed to be saying that her art had become a symbolic expression in which she could see and experience her feelings, mind, and body.

Eventually, Ms. A put together a portfolio of slides of her paintings, wrote cover letters, and began visiting galleries to show her artwork to gallery owners. She received and accepted an invitation to join a group of respected artists who met weekly and held some of the group's meetings in her home.

She told me that she was afraid she would lose her eyesight as she had lost use of her knee for dancing. But she added, "If I do lose my eyesight, I could try my hand at writing music."

Several years into the analysis, Ms. A decided to take a break to go to New York City and present to production companies some of the videotapes of dances she had choreographed. She felt that following through with this decision to take a break from analysis gave her a sense of freedom for the first time in her life, and she presented it to me with unwavering determination.

Ms. A's taking time off from analysis was a form of acting out, which did not surprise me because one side of her brand of resilience seemed to be defined in terms of the ability to take decisive action quickly. She was fleeing analysis for the streets of New York in part to reassure herself that she was not losing her edge, but she was also allowing herself to follow dreams that felt like her own, belonging neither to me, her mother, her father, nor anyone else.

When Ms. A returned to analysis 3 months later, she felt she had accomplished what she had set out to do. She said that she had realized while in New York that she still held out some hope that the dream house might actually exist somewhere. "In a way it's a relief to know it doesn't – all there is is what you see, so there's more if you can see more, but only up to a point and no more."

Discussion

As a resilient child, Ms. A had been to a considerable degree able to transcend the subjugating illness of her family. She was able to develop something of a life of her own and maintain her sanity without having to rely heavily on psychotic fragmentation, dissociation, or split-off pockets of psychosis [although she did engage in some powerful psychotic identifications (Searles, 1963/1965)].

What became clear as I worked with Ms. A was that one cannot completely escape the effects of trauma. To achieve a significant degree of psychological health in the face of trauma, one must not evade it but live in it, dream it, and think about it, thus making it one's own; putting one's personal mark on the experience.

Ms. A was largely able to remain vital, able to make psychological use of the best of what her family had to offer. For example, she was able to "help" her father at times to transcend the confines of the psychotic aspects of his personality sufficiently to make something of a healthy father-daughter relationship with her.

However, in her determination to wring more from her experiences than they, in fact, had to offer, Ms. A could become compulsive, driven, and in ways disconnected from external reality. For example, in her use of dance, she turned a potential for artistic use of bodily movement into a form of physically self-destructive acrobatics. Dancing, it seems to me, was a means for Ms. A to create and maintain an illusory early father-daughter relationship, and to strengthen her sense of body integrity. As such, dancing represented an intense (and doomed) effort to extract something good from something deeply flawed. So when her body failed, the illusory nature of much of her relationship with her father was exposed.

The patient's experiences with choreography and painting involved a shift to the use of talents that genuinely reflected her own unique psyche-soma. Through choreography, the patient seemed to be taking her place in her own generation. She was taking on a parental role with a give-and-take quality to it – using her creativity in a way that was not directly tied to unconscious conflicts with her father. Choreographers are the teachers of the next generation of dancers and, in this sense, are artistic parents to their students. Her choreography was a first attempt to step outside of the struggles of her unconscious internal object world to create and admire something of a genuine "not-me" experience.

As Ms. A began to sense the "otherness," the "not me" in the analytic relationship (for example, in her decision to take a break from analysis), she created a mind of her own in the act of choreographing and painting. Only with the patient's recognition of the "not me" – "the other" whom she could neither create nor destroy – was there psychological room for her to be not only creative but also a creative influence on others. She was able to marvel at and be genuinely surprised by what it felt like to take something in from another person and give it back in a transformed state (Schneider, 2003). In this period of analytic work, the dance, the art, became "the other" (transforming and transformed, but recognizable as itself); it became for Ms. A the experience of wonderment of the other as well as the frightening recognition of what was beyond her power to control or even to influence.

Ms. A feared that changing in the experience of the analysis would affect her creativity. I interpreted this fear as a fear of giving up her capacity "to get blood from a stone," which capacity had been essential for her in childhood.

The patient and I were able to recognize the inseparability of the health and the pathology of her resilience. She had become hypersensitive to external danger and unable to discriminate what threatened her survival from what was merely frustrating. In this way, her resilience involved making a lot from a little in a problematic fashion.

The anxiety associated with traumatic overwhelming psychic stimulation that was too powerful for Ms. A to manage (Freud, 1915/1957, 1920/1955, 1926/1959) led to her becoming highly sensitive to her environment and to her evacuating stimulation by means of bodily and other action-based maneuvers (Bion, 1962). By dissipating frustration in this way, she precluded transformation of raw sensory experience (beta elements) into perceptions linked with feelings and symbols and meaning-laden symbolic thought (alpha elements) suitable for storage as memory; rather, her conscious and unconscious experiences were denuded of meaning. In this way, they were rendered unavailable for fantasizing, dreaming, and other forms of conscious and unconscious psychological work.

In sum, Ms. A's remarkable self-preserving psychological resourcefulness in the face of severe neglect and abuse dating from early childhood was achieved at a considerable psychic cost. She came to analysis in response not only to trauma, but also in response to the pathology of her resilience. This pathology included the fact that, for her, virtually every situation that seemed to pose danger was responded to as if it were a matter of survival. Analysis itself was initiated as if her life depended on it (i.e., a response to suicidal feelings that she feared she would act on). In the analytic setting, Ms. A demonstrated fierce self-sufficiency and reluctance to become dependent upon me. At the outset, her need to wring every drop of sustenance from her life experience took a variety of forms including her making excessive demands on her own body, which resulted in the destruction of the connective tissue in her left knee.

Her resilience and its components were life-preserving in the face of severe traumatic experiences, but life-depleting when feeling, thinking, dreaming, and imagining were foreclosed in the interest of immediate recourse to anxiety-dissipating action. My work with Ms. A most fundamentally involved the analysis of the unconscious, Janus-faced nature of resilience.

Notes

1   Translation: "Whatever does not destroy me makes me stronger."
2   The English word "trauma" is derived from a Greek word meaning "wound" which is derived from "to pierce," and refers to any injury where the skin is broken as a consequence of external violence.
3   See Ogden (2003) and Grotstein (2002) for discussions of Bion's revisions to psychoanalytic theory regarding dreaming and "not being able to dream."
4   "Dreams" that are not dreams do not involve unconscious psychological work, and the dreamer is left psychically unchanged by them. Examples of dreams that are not dreaming include hallucinations, repetitive dreams following trauma, dreams that leave both patient

and analyst without associations to them, and imageless "dreams" that may involve a single uniform sound.

5   This "impression" was a form of background sensory awareness – not yet an image tethered to words and ideas or even a defined set of feelings.

References

Bion, W. R. (1962). *Learning from experience*. Basic Books.

Bion, W. R. (1967). *Second thoughts: A theory of thinking*. Jason Aronson.

Bion, W. R. (1970). *Attention and interpretation*. Tavistock Publications.

Freud, S. (1955). Beyond the pleasure principle. In J. Strachey (Ed. & Trans.), *Standard edition of the complete psychological works of Sigmund Freud* (Vol. 18, pp. 3–64). Hogarth Press. (Original work published (1920)

Freud, S. (1957). Instincts and their vicissitudes. In J. Strachey (Ed. & Trans.), *Standard edition of the complete psychological works of Sigmund Freud* (Vol. 14, pp. 105–140). Hogarth Press. (Original work published 1915)

Freud, S. (1959). Inhibitions, symptoms, and anxiety. In J. Strachey (Ed. & Trans.), *Standard edition of the complete psychological works of Sigmund Freud* (Vol. 20, pp. 77–175). Hogarth Press. (Original work published 1926)

Grotstein, J. S. (2000). *Who is the dreamer who dreams the dream? A study of psychic presences*. The Analytic Press.

Grotstein, J. S. (2002). "We are such stuff as dreams are made on" – Annotations on dreams and dreaming in Bion's works. In C. Neri, M. Pines, & R. Friedman (Eds.), *Dreams in group psychotherapy theory and technique*. Jessica Kingsley Publishers.

Nietzsche, F. W. (1889). *Twilight of the idols*.

Ogden, T. (2001). *Conversations at the frontiers of dreaming*. Jason Aronson.

Ogden, T. (2003). On not being able to dream. *International Journal of Psychoanalysis, 84*, 17–30.

Schneider, J. A. (1990). Gender identity issues in male bulimia nervosa. In C. Johnston (Ed.), *Psychodynamic treatments of anorexia nervosa and bulimia* (pp. 194–222). Guilford Press.

Schneider, J. A. (1995). Eating disorders, addictions, and unconscious fantasy. *Bulletin of the Menninger Clinic, 59*(2), 177–199.

Schneider, J. A. (2003). Working with pathological and healthy forms of splitting: A case study. *Bulletin of the Menninger Clinic, 67*(1), 32–49.

Searles, H. F. (1965). Transference psychosis in the psychotherapy of chronic schizophrenia. In *Collected papers on schizophrenia and related subjects* (Chap. 23). Hogarth Press Ltd. (Originally published 1963)

8

Eating Disorders, Addictions, and Unconscious Fantasy

The psychoanalytic understanding of eating disorders has revolved primarily around explanations generated by Freud (1905/1953), 1950/1966) and Bruch (1970, 1973, 1978). I believe that this understanding can be greatly enhanced by adding concepts of primitive, internal object relationships, as developed over the past 50 years by Fairbairn, Tustin, Ogden, and others.

I would like to contribute two concepts. The first idea, related to the compulsive and rhythmic nature of the binge-purge ritual, is that the experiences of eating disorder patients are sensation-dominated experiences located at the skin surface, which involve autistic shapes and objects (Ogden, 1989; Tustin, 1984, 1986). The autistic-contiguous position as defined by Ogden relates to pathological forms of unconscious defensive attachment to internal objects, and can be used to understand the transference and the countertransference of therapists treating eating disorder patients. The second idea, related to the addictive nature of eating disorders, is that the patient's attachment to the object reflects a futile unconscious fantasied quest that involves taking the bad object to transform it into good (Fairbairn, 1944/1952).

Theoretical Formulation

Freud conceptualized eating disorders of anorexia and bulimia as hysterical symptoms resulting from unconscious sexual conflict involving oral incorporative mechanisms and oedipal genital wishes. In 1899 (in his letters to Fliess), Freud (1950/1966) wrote that bulimia, or psychogenic vomiting, was representative of an underlying oral sadistic, cannibalistic sexual fantasy. This fantasy was that, from the young eating-disordered girl's point of view, she could eat her father's penis and be impregnated with his baby (Freud, 1905/1953). Psychogenic vomiting was the girl's neurotic, hysterical symptom resulting from this unconscious sexual conflict and subsequent compromise formation.

Freud's ideas were modified in the 1960s and 1970s by Bruch, who brought important elements into the discussion of eating disorders. Whereas Freud saw eating disorders as a conversion hysteria tied to oedipal issues, Bruch (1970, 1973, 1978) saw them as tied to preoedipal issues of separation and individuation. Bruch focused not on Freud's drive-conflict-defense model but instead on ego weaknesses and interpersonal

DOI:10.4324/9781003384601-8

disturbances that characterize eating disorder patients. She saw eating disorders not only as intrapsychic events but also as interpersonal events. They were expressions of the person's conflict between wanting to be a separate person and the wish to remain with the mother. Gender sameness helps to sustain the illusion that the girl and the mother are really one even if they are sometimes separated (Schneider, 1991).

To explain what she saw and heard from her patients, Bruch concluded that eating disorders did not involve oedipal problems or sexual interactions with the father but rather preoedipal problems of separation and autonomy from the mother, a mother who failed to respond appropriately. Bruch believed that the anorexic person's striving for thinness was an adaptive effort to separate herself from her mother. Bruch pointed out that eating disorder patients often have difficulty identifying or articulating internal states such as hunger, satiety, fullness, or emotions. Bruch also noted that most of her eating disorder patients were ineffective in their relationships with others.

This state of affairs continued until a new set of terms based on object-relations theory evolved from Freud's and Bruch's concepts. The work of Winnicott (1949/1975) and later McDougall (1974), to name two contributors, provides a framework for understanding eating disorders from an object-relations point of view. From this perspective, psychosomatic illnesses are a somatic expression of something the person cannot experience psychologically because it is not represented symbolically (McDougall, 1974). In this situation, the body gets exploited to express what the mind cannot, and it is an accomplice in the urgent instinctual discharge that bypasses psychic elaboration because of deficient symbolic representation.[1] According to Winicott (1949/1975), impingements from an imperfect environment are apprehended through the senses, resulting in an experience of deadness and a disturbance in the developing "continuity of being" (p. 245). Pathology results when the original psyche-soma partnership is replaced with a psyche-mind partnership. From the object-relations view, the sensory aspects of eating disorders are especially important in understanding how they function.

Ogden and Tustin

Ogden's (1989) autistic-contiguous position is a dimension of experience that seems to have particular importance for understanding eating disorders. It is based on his reinterpretation and elaboration of Klein (1958/1975), who offered a view of psychological development as a biphasic progression from the biological to the impersonal-psychological, and from the impersonal-psychological to the subjective. To explain how meaning is attributed to experience, Klein proposed two psychological positions (the paranoid-schizoid and the depressive), each of which has associated with it a particular quality of anxiety, form of object relatedness, and defense (Ogden, 1989).

It is essential to bear in mind that the autistic-contiguous position, like the paranoid-schizoid and depressive positions, does not occur as a pure entity. Positions are more like qualities of experience – like shape or color. They do not occur in pure form any more than color exists apart from shape. Rather, the experience exists as a whole.

We talk about a single quality or dimension of experience because all things cannot be spoken of at once. Each position has a cohesiveness, but it never constitutes the whole of every experience.

Eating disorder patients certainly use verbal symbols to organize experience, as suggested by the depressive position, and they certainly deal with projections, introjections, splitting, projective identifications, and symbolic equations, as suggested by the paranoid-schizoid position. (This position is a psychological organization generating a state of being where persons feel they are "lived by their experiences," and thoughts and feelings "just happen" instead of being thought or felt. An individual reacts automatically rather than responding.) I believe, however, that the autistic-contiguous position is also important in explaining how eating disorder patients assign meaning to an experience.

Before the period when the paranoid-schizoid position is predominant, there is a more primitive period (Ogden's autistic-contiguous position) having to do with attributing meaning to experience in which raw sensory data are ordered by forming presymbolic connections between sensory impressions and the experience of surfaces. Ogden (1989) suggested that "it is on these surfaces that the experience of self has its origins" (p. 49). This experience occurs before infants internalize objects. The infant's sense of continuity of being in this mode of experience is organized around sensory experience, particularly skin surface sensations, as well as rhythmicity. These sensory experiences form the earliest and most fundamental object relations, which are related to the infant's experience of being held, nursed, rocked, and spoken to by the mother.

Objects in this autistic-contiguous mode are not experienced as objects; instead, they are perceived in the form of relationships to autosensuous shapes (Tustin, 1984) and autosensuous objects (Tustin, 1980). Autistic *shapes* are "'felt' shapes" (Tustin, 1984, p. 280) that arise when the skin contacts a soft surface that makes sensory impressions on the skin's surfaces. Tustin (1984) suggested that we can create the experience of an autistic shape by mentally reducing the chair we are sitting on to the sensation it makes on our buttocks and back. Thus there is no sense of the chair as an object other than the sensation or sensory impression it makes. Ogden (1989) suggested that autistic shapes are predominantly experiences of soft objects, including soft parts of the mother's body, as well as soft parts of the infant's own body, such as skin, saliva, feces, and urine; and that in the autistic-contiguous mode of experience, words like "soothing" and "calming" become attached to experiences of shapes in this mode.

Tustin (1980) also defined autistic objects in contrast to autistic shapes. The characteristic feature of autistic objects is the experience of "hardness" created when the object touches the skin surface. Tustin suggested that this sensation is not localized to the place that is touched; rather, it is experienced by the infant as an armor for all the soft parts of the body necessary for bodily survival and protection from annihilation. This "pseudoprotection" becomes a substitute for connection with human beings, and it arises when the skin contacts a hard surface and creates an internal vault where caring from others cannot get in and one's needs for people cannot get out. Ogden (1986) suggested that the infant experiences an autistic object as a safety-generating sensory impression of "edgedness" that defines, delineates, and protects its otherwise exposed and vulnerable surfaces.

Of special importance to this discussion is that relationships with autistic shapes and objects are "perfect" in that they lie outside the unpredictability of relationships with human beings and can be replicated precisely the same way whenever they are needed. They remain exactly the same for the whole life.

Ogden (1989) described the characteristic manifestation of autistic-contiguous anxiety to include terrifying feelings that one is rotting; the sensation that one's sphincters and other means of containing bodily contents are failing and that one's saliva, tears, urine, feces, blood, menstrual fluids, and so forth are leaking; fear that one is falling – for example, anxiety connected with falling asleep for fear that one will fall into endless, shapeless space. (p. 68)

Defenses against loss of sensory boundedness and leaking uncontrollably through holes in the skin may take the form of what Bick (1968, 1986) called the "formation of a . . . 'second skin'" (1968, p. 485), an alternative to holding the personality together where no internal containing object has been established.

According to Bick (1968, 1986), the most fundamental fear characterizing the infant's existence is fear of self-annihilation. Meltzer (1975) introduced the concept of "adhesive identification" to describe the defensive sticking to an object at the surface level to safeguard against the anxiety of disintegration and the use of imitation and mimicry in place of identification. Dependence on the object is replaced with pseudoindependence. The formation of a "second skin" is the individual's attempt to provide a sense of self – to hold the unintegrated parts of the self together where no sense of the self exists. Later, as an adult, the person manifests this fear in the transference in psychoanalysis as problems with dependence and separation, particularly around changes in the day-to-day routine of the relationship (e.g., between sessions, on weekends, or during breaks in therapy).

Infants have an unconscious fantasied quest to achieve wholeness by attaching to "autistic shapes," and – literally and figuratively – they compulsively repair leaks in their sensory self. For eating disorder patients, the sense that their life depends on the fulfillment of this impossible quest leads to the compulsive and repetitive nature of their experience. I believe it is the compulsive and rhythmic nature of the binge-purge ritual that becomes the external "glue" to hold these persons together and sustain them.

Fairbairn

Ogden's (1989) and Tustin's (1980, 1984) sensation-based models complement and supplement Fairbairn's (1944/1952) internal object-relations theory. Fairbairn's theory has to do with object-representations and an internal world that is in need of Ogden's and Tustin's sensation theory to explain the most primitive aspect of the schizoid personality. Likewise, Ogden's and Tustin's sensation theory is part of Fairbairn's object-relations theory and needs a place in it to make it complete. The sensation-dominated autistic shapes and objects were recognized by Ogden (1989) as the "soft underbelly" or precursors to Fairbairn's internal object-relations theory.

> The schizoid condition can be thought of as Janus-faced: one face directed with fear and longing to the external object world that lies beyond the reach of the patient's illusions/delusions of omnipotence; the other face directed to sensory-dominated state more primitive than that connected with the internal object world envisioned by Klein and Fairbairn. The latter "face" is the inarticulate underbelly of schizoid experience in which phantasy gives way to presymbolic, sensory-dominated experience.
>
> (Ogden, 1989, p. 87)

Fairbairn's object-relations theory, specifically the concept of taking in the bad object to control it and make it good, helps explain the addictive nature of eating disorders. Fairbairn (1944/1952) proposed that the infant is born with a hypothetically whole ego (i.e., the self) in relation to a theoretically whole object. Immediately after birth, the infant is presented with the external reality of the mother and with the realization that the mother is not able to replicate the pleasant and preferable intrauterine state. This situation leads to a splitting of the ego into good and bad components. From then on, of necessity, the infant must relate to both the satisfying and unsatisfying object. According to Fairbairn, there is no reason to internalize the good object; rather, only if the infant feels that the mother has failed to provide satisfaction is it necessary to internalize the bad-object mother.

The purpose of internalizing the bad object is so the infant can control it to turn it into a good object. Thus the bad object is internalized from outer reality, and the relationship to the bad object is angrily repressed. Ties between these parts of the self and the object are love-hate ties – united in anger and hate, as well as in love and dependence.

Fairbairn assumed that humans are most fundamentally object related, and that the need for other humans is more deeply felt than the need for water, food, or sex. Thus no human being, no matter how good or bad, will be discarded. If the mother is experienced as bad, the infant holds on to her and constantly attempts to rework her, taking her in and then discarding her in futile attempts to make her good. The individual continually relates to the hated or rejecting object because bad objects are better than no objects. There is an attachment to the bad, hated mother that fuels the addiction. Out-of-control bulimic individuals are spitefully feeding the hated self inside, who is imagined to have an insatiable appetite. It is their own hated version of themselves, identified with their mother's feeding them. The food becomes a self-imposed "oral rape." In the same way that rape is not about sex but is instead a sexual form of, or medium for, hatred, in some cases, the "eating" binge has more to do with aggression than with food or hunger.

In the case of eating disorders, the relationship to the bad object becomes an addictive, relentless attempt to get love, which clearly cannot be obtained. The symptoms become repetitive attempts by the individual to take in the bad object to control it and then to get rid of it through binging and purging.

The addictive quality of eating disorders is related to a fantasy that one's life depends on completing a certain unconscious fantasied act or quest. This unconscious fantasied quest may take various manifest behavior forms, such as, for example, when a person compulsively attempts to gain the mother's love by repeatedly inducing a drugged state of mind, or by making such-and-such an amount of money, or by writing such-and-such number of books, or by achieving in some other highly driven way. The addicted activity is compulsively repeated in reality and in the object relations of the person.

I believe that for the eating disorder patient, the unconscious fantasied quest is, in Fairbairn's terms, the transformation of the internal bad-object mother into a good object. This unconscious quest, upon which the person's life depends for completion, is by definition unattainable, because the person cannot change the past. The mother cannot be made to be more loving in the way one wishes she would have been. What the individual can do, however, is to come to grips with who the mother was and what the person could not accept from her – but one can never redo or undo her. The past is not going to be changed. The quest will never be brought to completion, but the person can change his or her relationship to the quest itself.

With this theoretical background, I will now clinically illustrate some of the ways that these ideas from object-relations theory can enhance understanding of an eating disorder patient. In this case, I address the autistic-contiguous experiences of the patient related to transference and countertransference issues. In addition, the case illustrates how Fairbairn's object-relations theory helps us understand the addictive behavior of the patient, and how the patient moves from the autistic-contiguous position to the threshold of the paranoid-schizoid position.

Clinical Illustration

Mr. K, a 34-year-old unmarried man with whom I worked for many years, came to me because he had spent his life bingeing and vomiting – sometimes up to 40 times a day. Mr. K, who worked as a data specialist, was comfortable with the technical language of mathematics, but he spent only a few hours each day at his job because he usually stopped on his way to work at a string of restaurants to binge on huge meals. At night, Mr. K stayed up bingeing and vomiting, afraid to fall asleep, sometimes getting only a few hours of sleep each night. When he came to see me, he suffered from gum disease, and 75% of his teeth had been destroyed by the incessant stomach acid wash from purging.

During our first meeting, he periodically touched his hand to a bulge in his side pants pocket. Near the end of the meeting, he removed a wad of hundreds of business cards, asking for mine in the process. These cards, dirty and tattered, served as autistic objects for Mr. K. He kept them close to his skin; their edges and uniform shape were always available, and there was always another to replace one that had fallen apart.

Mr. K told me that the only time he felt warm and alive was when he was eating. When he ate, he could sense his body chemistry changing, his blood flowing into his skin, and his body temperature rising. He teetered on the brink of death, making a game of predicting the level of his chronic low potassium level. When he was not eating, he purposely kept himself very cold.

Mr. K was an only child. His father traveled extensively and was away for long periods. When he was home, he was verbally and physically abusive, which kept Mr. K tied to his mother. The mother, a depressed and isolated woman, told her son that his father was a "no-good," a liar. Mr. K felt he always had to be near his mother, even though he experienced her as "always poking at me."

When Mr. K was 6 years old, his father died of colon cancer at home after a 2-year illness. During the illness, Mr. K's mother told him not to enter his father's room. But one day he sneaked in to see his father and was appalled and disgusted to find that he had wasted away to almost nothing.

As he grew up, Mr. K imitated his father's emaciated and dead state by keeping himself cold, unfeeling, and thin, in a wasted state near death. He felt comforted by the bodily sensations associated with his near-death state. Feeling alive through being human was not enough; he needed to heighten his skin sensations in his near-death rituals to feel alive. Mr. K had difficulty separating from his mother, and after he moved to California, he still telephoned her in New York almost daily.

Mr. K's case illustrates the importance of sensory aspects of eating disorders, the lack of an internal sense of self, and dependence on autistic objects. It also shows the feeling that one's survival and rudimentary experience depend on completing an unconscious fantasied quest underlying eating disorders, that of relating to the "bad object" in an addictive way to get love by changing the bad into good. Mr. K seemed to evidence an attachment to sensory objects that eating disorder patients display. He said he felt alive only when he was bingeing and purging. At other times he feared "I might just disappear, and float into space." He also feared that he had an ulcer that was rotting a hole in his stomach, and that his insides would leak out if he kept anything in his stomach.

Mr. K used bingeing and vomiting to provide himself with sensations that comforted him and reduced his anxiety. His routine of binging and purging followed a sequence of steps that was completely predictable, and to which he could relate autistically. In the same way that the rhythmicity of rocking is a predictable and comforting sensation, so too was his binging and purging ritual.

When he binged, Mr. K focused on the sensations of warm blood flowing through his skin. These sensations at his skin surface and the predictable routine were the essential elements of his bingeing and vomiting. He was terrified of feeling the sensation of fullness in his stomach, terrified that he would explode. He existed primarily in the autistic-contiguous world of external sensations rather than in a world of symbolic fantasy.

While he binged, Mr. K read, keeping his eyes focused on the reading material, even though he comprehended little of what he was reading. He told me he read "anything I can get my hands on" while he was bingeing, without regard to its content. Reading was a sensory activity, not an intellectual activity. He did not follow the story or character development but was totally absorbed in the sensory act of reading, much as a child listening to a bedtime story is more involved with the sound of the parent's voice than with the story itself and delights in hearing the story over and over again.

From the beginning, Mr. K tried to relate to me and the treatment as autistic objects. For our first meeting, he was late and called me from a telephone booth, saying he wanted to conduct the rest of the therapy session by phone. During the initial phase of treatment, there were other times when he tried to replace our sessions in person with sessions by telephone. He pleaded and whined for me to allow him to call me any time he wished.

In keeping me at a distance and connecting to me only by telephone, he could relate to me as part of his fantasy world – an extension of his wish to attach and detach at will, as he did with food. Rather than relating to me in person as an external object, by using the phone, he reduced me to an autistic shape, there at his creation.

Initially, I interpreted this behavior as representing a part-object relationship involving omnipotent control over me, and an introjective process that could be more controlled by him. Although this interpretation describes an aspect of the experience, it was also understandable in terms of his reducing me to the sensory experience of the sound of my voice and the sensation of the phone receiver against his ear. Another layer of safety was provided by the shell/skin of the phone booth. This interpretation seemed more accurate because later in treatment, he told me that the sound of my voice was comforting to him and that he wanted to extend sessions so he could continue listening to me. His being calmed by my voice seemed to illustrate an autistic attachment to it.

Early in treatment, his common refrain (which he screamed at me) was, "I have no thoughts, no more thoughts! I've shot my wad! Why won't you interact with me?" Mr. K could not hold internal objects or sustain them inside because there was no internal environment to hold things. Rather, his internal environment needed to be resuscitated continually, like an infant who can sleep only as long as it is held by its mother. The baby is not able to internalize a holding state in which it can hold itself and sleep, and so it wakes up constantly.

Mr. K's autistic mode of experiencing was also evidenced by the difficulty he had in going to sleep. In several of our meetings, he described his nightly routine of staying up all night bingeing and vomiting, with the TV blaring. This activity enabled him to fall asleep from exhaustion for an hour or two around dawn. I then said to him, "I think you fear falling asleep because by falling asleep, you fear you will dissolve into nothingness." The next day when he returned for his session, he slept for almost the entire hour. When he awoke, he said he felt rested in a way he could not remember feeling. It was as if he had used me and the therapy setting as a comforting, protective, and containing skin that could prevent him from leaking into space.

Another aspect of Mr. K's relating to me can best be described by Meltzer's (1975) concept of "adhesive identification." This relationship was particularly evident when Mr. K began pleading for extra minutes at the end of the hour and wondering if we could not "piggyback" another hour onto the one just completed. I felt extreme pressure being with him, as if we were floating aimlessly in space, with him clinging to me parasitically for survival. His need to remain with me at the end of sessions made me feel that he was stuck to me and that I would have to peel him off with my fingers like I would peel off a skin, or a wet suit.

As treatment progressed over the years, Mr. K seemed to teeter between the autistic-contiguous mode of sensation-based experience and a paranoid-schizoid world of internalized, persecutory objects. This fluctuation was illustrated in his reaction to holiday separations during treatment. Mr. K feared he would "disintegrate – just vanish," and he became desperate to repair the break he felt in his skin surface. Prior to a break, he left a telephone message requesting "a few extra minutes" before and after our next meeting. During the meeting, he told me he wanted to go to the hospital during my absence. He did not trust himself to stay alive. He wanted to replace therapy with hospitalization, thinking the hospital would be a safe place where he could find comfort while I was away – a "second skin" not unlike his felt need for the telephone booth at the beginning of treatment.[2]

The threat of separating from me precipitated Mr. K's addiction to watching endless hours of a late-night TV show called *Hill Street Blues*. He watched repetitive reruns until he knew the plots and dialogue from memory. When another show replaced this program, he was so upset by the loss of his show that he called the station, obtained the producer's home telephone number, and called him at midnight, ranting and raving about his missed show. He seemed to be acting as if his life support system had been turned off.

Because he knew the program so well, Mr. K related to the characters as autistic shapes who were completely controllable, dependable, and predictable to him. He found the characters soothing and calming and experienced their loss as devastating. I said to him, "I understand that it's been very upsetting to interrupt the treatment while I'm away, and that it's brought back a lot of feelings about the trouble you get into when you rely on someone. It isn't like relying on late-night TV. The trouble with human beings is that you can't predict what's going to happen, and there would be something wonderfully comforting if I were a TV show that you could turn on and watch every night. I'd be perfectly reliable, and you wouldn't have to get involved with all this junk about my leaving."

It was not the content of the show that Mr. K found soothing, but rather the predictability of it, and the way he could attach to it adhesively. This sensation was what caused him to feel so upset when the show was replaced. The loss of the show was not about the loss of an object but about the sense of a hole being torn in him. The separation anxiety he felt when the show was removed was experienced in a persecutory form, with images of the producer halting the show to terrify him.

The paranoid-schizoid dimension of his experience served to concretize it and was used as a defense against the autistic-contiguous anxiety of his leaking away and dissolving into nothingness. This understanding was dramatically illustrated in one episode where, after a meeting with me on Friday in which he felt particularly satisfied and alive at the end of the hour, he went home and ate several meals that he did not purge. After a short time, he was terrified. He left me a message that he was in a state of emergency. When I talked to him at our next meeting, he said that he had kept down the meals but his breath smelled like gasoline and he was afraid he would explode.

As this episode illustrates, Mr. K had good reason not to feel alive; when he came alive, he was alive in what he experienced as a persecutory world. When he experienced internal objects, they were terrifying. This was also seen in his dreams. When he began treatment, Mr. K told me he had less than one dream a year. As the treatment evolved, he said he had begun to remember his dreams, but they were full of people persecuting him. For instance, in one dream he was nailed to a cross. At the start of his work with me, perhaps his dreams were sensation dreams that did not take the usual form of visual imagery and symbolic representation. As treatment progressed, he experienced being alive more in the paranoid-schizoid position.

Discussion

Mr. K's case illustrates the autistic-contiguous aspects of severe eating disorders and how they affect the transference and countertransference. Soon after I began working with Mr. K, it became clear that he expected me to keep him alive; yet I did not exist for him, and he did not allow a place for me. His transference did not center around projecting onto me various internal objects so that I became mean or jealous. It was more a sense of being ignored, as if I were not present. There was little in his internal object world beyond what was created in our meetings; hence, he demanded to extend them and to have me available whenever he wished. The nature of Mr. K's transference was to the "matrix of transference" (Winnicott, 1958/1965a, p. 33; see also Ogden, 1991), so in speaking to him, I was not a representation of the mother as object but rather of the "environmental mother" (Winnicott, 1963/1965b, p. 182). In the absence of internal objects, Mr. K transferred his experience of his internal environment to the analytic setting that we created.

Initially, Mr. K was not just devoid of a sense of inner space; instead, the surface was all there was. The surface was not superficial to anything else; there was no inside. As with the skin surface of the infant and mother touching, the issue was not, "Is it inside or outside?" Rather, the experience was the sensation of the two coming together. Mr. K's repetitive activities of bingeing and purging were efforts to heighten the skin surface feelings in an attempt to get the sensations inside, to cross the barrier of the "second skin."

Mr. K was not able to take in via introjection, and thus he was not able to project affects. His was a pre-affect experience because there was no "he" and no "himself." Similarly, his conception of relationships was that they were external; he believed that others related only to his external self. His use of imitation rather than identification resulted in his feeling that he needed to be in my presence to hold himself together.

Mr. K did not appear to be using projective identification in relating to me.[3] I believe he was using something more primitive. It felt more like a folie a deux.[4] We were two people sharing the same delusional experience – actually, a lack of experience – because there was no mind or fantasy for creating meaning.

Mr. K felt as though breaks in treatment at the end of the hour or during longer separations "tore a hole in me." He demanded longer treatment sessions as a way to close the holes he felt were opened by allowing himself to be involved with me. At these and other times, I felt extreme, burning fatigue – a fatigue I became aware of only during and after I met him.

Notes

1 It was Freud (1923/1961) who first wrote that the self has its origins in the body: "The ego is first and foremost a bodily ego" (p. 26). Later he wrote that "the ego is ultimately derived from bodily sensations, chiefly from those springing from the surface of the body" (p. 26, footnote added in 1927).
2 It is noteworthy that, over his lifetime, Mr. K had been hospitalized 20 times. Once in the hospital, he immediately became symptom free and a model patient, enjoying the predictable nature of the care he got there. The institution became a protective umbrella – a "second skin."
3 Projective identification is a defense often used in the paranoid-schizoid position, but also seen in the depressive and autistic-contiguous positions. As a defense against anxiety of an autistic-contiguous nature, projective identification would involve evacuation of internal experience with very little symbolic representation, even in symbolic equation. It is more likely to be somatic in nature, thus leaving the projector feeling disconnected and floating in space.
4 The presence of the same or similar delusional ideas in two persons closely associated with one another.

References

Bick, E. (1968). The experience of the skin in early object-relations. *International Journal of Psychoanalysis, 49*, 484–486.
Bick, E. (1986). Further considerations on the function of the skin in early object relations: Findings from infant observation integrated into child and adult analysis. *British Journal of Psychotherapy, 2*, 292–299.
Bruch, H. (1970). Psychotherapy in primary anorexia nervosa. *Journal of Nervous and Mental Disease, 150*, 51–67.
Bruch, H. (1973). *Eating disorders: Obesity, anorexia nervosa, and the person within*. Basic Books.
Bruch, H. (1978). *The golden cage*. Harvard University Press.
Fairbairn, W. R. D. (1952). Endo-psychic structure considered in terms of object-relationships. In *Psychoanalytic studies of the personality*. Routledge & Kegan Paul. (Original work published 1944).
Freud, S. (1953). Three essays on the theory of sexuality. In J. Strachey (Ed. & Trans.), *Standard edition of the complete psychological works of Sigmund Freud* (Vol. 7, pp. 123–245). Hogarth Press. (Original work published 1905)
Freud, S. (1961). The ego and the id. In J. Strachey (Ed. & Trans.), *Standard edition of the complete psychological works of Sigmund Freud* (Vol. 19, pp. 1–66). Hogarth Press. (Original work published 1923)
Freud, S. (1966). Extracts from the Fliess papers. In J. Strachey (Ed. & Trans.), *Standard edition of the complete psychological works of Sigmund Freud* (Vol. 1, pp. 175–280). Hogarth Press. (Original work published 1950)
Klein, M. (1975). On the development of mental functioning. In *Envy and gratitude and other works: 1946–1963*. Free Press. (Original work published 1958)
McDougall, J. (1974). The psycho-soma and the psychoanalytic process. *International Review of Psychoanalysis, 1*, 437–459.
Meltzer, D. (1975). Adhesive identification. *Contemporary Psychoanalysis, 11*, 289–310.
Ogden, T. H. (1986). *The matrix of the mind: Object relations and the psychoanalytic dialogue*. Aronson.

Ogden, T. H. (1989). *The primitive edge of experience*. Aronson.

Ogden, T. H. (1991). Analyzing the matrix of transference. *International Journal of Psychoanalysis, 72*, 593–605.

Schneider, J. A. (1991). Gender identity issues in male bulimia nervosa. In C. L. Johnson (Ed.), *Psychodynamic treatment of anorexia nervosa and bulimia*. Guilford.

Schneider, J. A., O'Leary, A., & Jenkins, S. R. (1995). Gender, sexual orientation, and disordered eating. *Psychology and Health, 10*, 113–128.

Tustin, F. (1980). Autistic objects. *International Review of Psychoanalysis, 7*, 27–39.

Tustin, F. (1984). Autistic shapes. *International Review of Psychoanalysis, 11*, 279–290.

Tustin, F. (1986). *Autistic barriers in neurotic patients*. Yale University Press.

Winnicott, D. W. (1965a). The capacity to be alone. In *The maturational processes and the facilitating environment: Studies in the theory of emotional development*. International Universities Press. (Original work published 1958)

Winnicott, D. W. (1965b). Communicating and not communicating leading to a study of certain opposites. In *The maturational processes and the facilitating environment: Studies in the theory of emotional development*. International Universities Press. (Original work published 1963)

Winnicott, D. W. (1975). Mind and its relation to the psycho-soma. In *Collected papers: Through paediatrics to psychoanalysis*. Basic Books. (Original work published 1949)

9

Signs and Symbols in *Dersu Uzala*

Dersu Uzala, the 1975 film directed by Akira Kurosawa, the renowned Japanese film-maker, in conjunction with Russia's Mosfilm Studios, presents a seemingly simple human drama played out in an uncharted area of Siberia. With a screenplay based on Vladimir Arseniev's 1941 nonfiction account of his experience with a nomadic trapper, *Dersu Uzala* was Kurosawa's second color movie and his first movie outside Japan with non-Japanese actors.

The narrating voice we hear is that of Captain Vladimir Arseniev, a Russian geographer and cartographer, as he writes a memoir of two surveying expeditions in the rugged Siberian wilderness, the Ussurian taiga. Arseniev tells the story in a series of flashbacks of his days with Dersu Uzala, a man who lived in this remote region and with whom he formed an uncommon friendship. The movie traces this friendship and its effects on both men – one a cultured, well-educated scientist and military officer, the other a mountain man living alone in the forest in one of the world's harshest environments.

The story of these two men and the complex emotional bond they form is told against a backdrop of spectacular natural beauty, with the changes of seasons in Siberia echoing the changes in their relationship. The film is a panoramic vision – like a series of beautiful photographs, each capturing the colors and textures of nature untouched by humankind. The camera focuses steadily on expansive scenes so that they appear to be still shots, moving only enough to capture the global movements of the characters. Because there are few close-ups of the characters, the human drama seems insignificant in relation to the eternal cycles of the natural world. Indeed, nature is one of the characters in the film: the powerful beauty of the Siberian landscape speaks for itself. This contrasts with some of Kurosawa's earlier movies propelled by rapid, often-furious editing in which action often ended in violence. Here, Kurosawa sets the tone with superb cinematography, as in the opening scenes in which the camera leisurely pans the Siberian landscape with its brilliant autumn foliage of oranges, yellows, and reds, as a bird shrieks in the distance.

The tranquil opening scene gives way to a scene of confusion in 1910 Korfovskaya, Siberia, as Captain Arseniev (Yuri Salomin) looks for the grave of Dersu Uzala (Maxim Munzuk). The scene is one of bustling business while a new settlement is carved out of the forest. Arseniev wanders about, lost and discouraged amid the chaotic desecration

DOI:10.4324/9781003384601-9

of the wilderness and his friend's resting place. Despairing of finding the grave and left only with his memories, Arseniev wistfully says his friend's name, "Dersu."

In a flashback to 1902, Captain Arseniev, weary and walking with a slight left-leg limp, leads his military survey team of about a dozen men through a barren wilderness. At night the men are awakened by what sounds like an approaching bear. After a few tense moments during which the soldiers arm themselves, a small, wizened, bow-legged man walks calmly into camp and greets the captain as if they were old friends.

The soldiers acknowledge that Dersu is not a bear; yet his weathered face, rugged clothes, and rough manner make it clear that Dersu is not an ordinary man. After Dersu has settled himself near the fire, he lights his pipe – an odd, slightly comic sight, as if a bear were enjoying a smoke.

Dersu explains that he came across the tracks of the soldiers and followed the men to the camp. Clearly he had been watching the soldiers for some time before he joined them. When Arseniev offers Dersu food, he eats hungrily, without conversing, in an un-self-conscious manner closer to the ways of animals than to those of men.

Dersu, of the Manchurian branch of the Tungus-Manchurian tribe, is one of only 5,000 remaining hunters and fishermen who live in the remote Russian territory. He is without a home and without a family – his wife, son, and daughter died of smallpox years earlier. After their deaths, Dersu burned the house with their bodies in it and began his life alone in the wilderness.

When the soldiers ask Dersu his age, he ponders the question and admits he does not know but that he has lived a long time. Outside of "man-made" time, Dersu lives in natural time, governed by the cycles of the seasons, of prey and predator, of drought and floods.

Captain Arseniev, recognizing Dersu's strength and wisdom and his visceral knowledge of the forest, invites him to be their guide. Quixotically, Dersu says he needs to think it over. Though he has lived apart from other human beings and has shunned civilization for most of his life, he has not been able to escape his own humanity. Pulled by an inner imperative to rejoin the human race for reasons he does not understand, he agrees to guide the soldiers.

Initially, the soldiers laugh and poke fun at Dersu as paw prints and broken branches give him direction, and steam rising from bogs forecasts the weather. As his predictions are repeatedly borne out, the soldiers begin to view with awe his capacity to read nature's signs. Having discovered a makeshift hut in the wilderness, Dersu repairs the roof with bark and then asks the captain for salt and matches, which he leaves in the newly repaired hut. When asked if he plans to return, Dersu replies no, that it's for the next person to come. Men, like Dersu, have superimposed their own cycles on those of nature.

Fully aware of the power of nature, Dersu knows that he is an insignificant part of it. He lives a form of animism by which he imparts a spirit to all things. He refers to fire, water, and wind as "three mighty men" and the sun as "the most important man." Dersu is part of a myth that he does not view as myth (i.e., as symbolic). By joining the soldiers, Dersu risks being torn out of the myth and becoming stranded alone in a world of symbols he cannot read.

Dersu's is a world in which the nature of reality is intertwined with imagination, dreams, and spirit. He does not wake up from his dreams – dreamlife is continuous with waking life. In one scene, he chants and makes offerings to wood he's burning; his shouts are answered by the screams of a bird. Dersu later tells the captain that he had a dream the previous night. In his dream, the yurt was shaking and was about to fall down. His wife and kids were in the yurt hungry and cold, so he had come to give them some food. For Dersu, the spirit continues after death and can be kept alive; in effect, there is no death.

In another wilderness scene, the expedition encounters an old Chinese man sitting on his haunches, rocking in the doorway of a hut. The captain makes him an offering of water and bread, but the man is so disturbed when aroused from his stupor that he shakes violently, spilling the water. Dersu tells the captain that Li Tsung-Ping is 64 years old and for 40 years has lived alone in the wilderness after his brother stole his woman from him. Later, when the captain wants to invite Li Tsung-Ping to their campfire, Dersu tells the captain not to disturb the old man – to leave him alone with his thoughts. In this way Dersu seems to acknowledge the danger to which he exposes himself as a result of his growing ties to the captain. He risks being awakened from his animal-like dreamlife to face a human awareness of the pain of irreversible loss (Schneider, 2005a, 2005b, 2007) – an awareness of death that is absolute and devoid of the endless cycles of nature.

A critical turning point in the film occurs when, despite Dersu's warnings, the captain insists that they go alone to the frozen Lake Khanka. They get lost in a blizzard as night sets in because Arseniev is so taken by the beauty of the lake that he cannot tear himself away. At the same time as the captain seems to become one with nature, Dersu is beginning to emerge from being part of it. Completely lost, they trudge in circles. Dersu warns that after dark they will be finished.

Knowing every moment counts, Dersu takes charge, ordering the captain to cut grass and work fast. Together they feverishly cut reeds. But soon Arseniev loses consciousness, succumbing to cold and exhaustion. Using the tripod for a canopy holder, Dersu fashions a reed tent around the captain and himself.

In the morning, Dersu delivers the captain from the shelter. As he removes the life-saving reeds, he playfully refers to the captain as a bear and invites him to climb out of his den, saying the sun is up. The two men give each other bear hugs and gleefully roll on the snow-covered ground. It is as if the two have met at that precise place that arches the border between Dersu's dawning of human consciousness and Arseniev's entry into an un-self-conscious world of nature.

They seem to have given birth to one another – each giving something essential (and yet potentially very dangerous) to the other. Dersu delivers the captain to the world of raw, sensual, nonsymbolic rapturous union with nature that involved a close scrape with death. The emotionally reserved captain freely expresses joyful, unmediated elation, frolicking like a bear cub in the snow. The captain seems to have been drawn by a force stronger than human will into the nonhuman world. No longer is wilderness only terrain to be symbolized by maps and subdued by civilization. Conversely, the captain delivers Dersu into the world of self-conscious humanity, and of human bonds – intimacy and friendship of a uniquely human sort.

In the final scene of Part I, as the men discuss their plans, it is evident that Dersu and the captain must part. The captain asks Dersu to come with him to the city, but Dersu refuses. Sensing Dersu's need to continue living alone, the captain offers him food and money, but Dersu asserts that he needs nothing (and no one). Before they part, he asks the captain for a few cartridges, a concession of sorts. The captain orders the soldiers to give to Dersu all their extra cartridges. The paradox is poignant: Dersu refuses to enter the human symbolic realm, but he is unable fully to resist.

As the scene ends, we see Dersu and the men parting at the recently constructed railroad track, which is now a gleaming steel line separating Dersu and Arseniev. When Dersu reaches the top of a hill, he turns back. He and the captain look at each other from the distance and fondly call out to each other, "Dersu," and in reply, "Captain."

Part II of the film begins 5 years later in the spring of 1907. Arseniev is again leading a surveying expedition. The soldiers are contending with the forces of Siberia's spring thaw, slogging through waist-deep mud. The river heaves and cracks as ice breaks and huge chunks grind against one another in the torrent.

The captain has spent 3 months in the forest clearly hoping to run into Dersu when finally a soldier reports that he met a hunter in the woods who asked about their unit. The captain runs in the direction from which the soldier came, calling "Dersu"; and, shortly, in the distance, the reply, "Captain!"

As they rush toward each other, a huge fallen tree separates them. They run back and forth along the two sides of the fallen trunk, panting and laughing, calling each other's name, looking each other in the eye, and trying to touch each other. Then, in one of the most poignant scenes of the film, they meet at the end of the trunk and grab hold of one another, the captain hugging Dersu's head to his breast. Later, Dersu and Arseniev sit off to the side of the main campfire, sharing stories and laughing, while the men sing a song, perhaps a serenade for the reunited lovers.

Their reunion is clearly more than a simple meeting of old friends. Beyond the bond of friendship, the two men seem to have found in one another aspects of themselves that each of them has not fully experienced or expressed before. In finding Dersu again, the captain seems to have gained something essential to his vitality that he finds nowhere else. Similarly, Dersu is no longer fulfilled by his solitary life in the wilderness.

Eventually Dersu's old age and failing health make him vulnerable and insecure. Along the trail, Dersu sees the tracks of a Siberian tiger stalking them. Later they see the tiger, and Dersu yells at it to go away, but it comes toward them. He shoots at it to warn it off, but then, as it races away, he drops his gun in shocked remorse and fears that he has harmed something sacred to Kanga – the spirit of the forest – who will now send another tiger to kill him. By joining the expedition, he has entered human time, with its endings dictated by death. Dersu is now a weakened and doomed human in the animal world.

From that day on, Dersu becomes morose and irritable. Coming upon a stag, the captain urges Dersu to shoot it, but the old man's eyes fail him, and he misses. Believing that Dersu is too old and frail to continue living in the forest, the captain invites him to come and live with him in the city of Khabarovsk.

Dersu's fear of dying peaks on New Year's Eve in the camp. A tiger passes by Dersu's tent, and, in terror, he throws burning sticks at it and yells that the tiger has come to kill him. He believes Kanga doesn't want him to live in the forest because Kanga sent the tiger. Dersu then thanks the captain for offering his home to him and agrees to go to Khabarovsk.

Because Dersu has reentered the world of human connection and the inevitability of loss, the formerly revered tiger takes on a sinister meaning symbolizing Dersu's death. Dersu has found himself stranded outside of the myth in which he had been living. Prominently placed between the captain and Dersu, the tiger is the embodiment of Dersu's conflicted awakening to human self-consciousness.

Once in Khabarovsk, Dersu is restless, looking like a caged animal. He feels confined in the house and wants to pitch a tent outside – symbolic of his futile wish to re-enter his wilderness dream state. Once out, it seems he can never return. He is neither a man with dignity nor an animal with cunning. Finally, Dersu pleads with the captain to let him go back to the hills. He says he can't live in a city because he can't breathe there. The captain, who is at a loss to know how to make his friend happy, gets a new rifle and gives it to Dersu, telling him it is easy to aim even with bad eyesight. Dersu returns to the wilderness with the rifle.

In the penultimate scene, Arseniev receives a telegram saying that his visiting card was found on a dead Goldi and his presence was requested to identify the body to the police at the Koorkovsk Railway Station. Arseniev travels by train to Koorkovsk to identify Dersu's body, which is being buried next to the railroad tracks. When the officer in charge asks if he knew him, Arseniev responds that they were friends, and his friend's name was Dersu Uzala, and his occupation was as a hunter. The officer mentions how strange it was that Dersu did not have a rifle. Arseniev assures him there must have been a rifle, one of the latest models, because he gave it to him. But the officer says no rifle was found and speculates that someone killed Dersu for his fine rifle. Arseniev is stricken by the sad irony of Dersu's death – a human killing utterly disconnected from the timeless cycles of nature.

The film ends as it began, with Arseniev mourning the loss of Dersu. At the grave, we hear the same music that the soldiers earlier sang as a serenade to the two reunited friends. The words of the song reflect the fate of the friendship: "My gray wing'd eagle – where have you gone?" The chorus replies: "I'm flying . . ." "You, my eagle with blue black wings, where have you been flying for so long" – "I was flying there over the mountains – where it all was silence."

We are left with the questions ever-present in this film: What is it to be a man, to be a human, to be an animal, to know one is mortal, to love other men and be loved by them, to retain one's nonhuman animal nature, to be a good man?

In 1971, after Kurosawa experienced two film failures – he attempted suicide by slashing himself multiple times with a razor. Following his physical recovery, however, he assumed a different persona. He was more affable and social, granting interviews with the news media, in stark contrast to his earlier, reclusive self. Shortly thereafter, finding no interest in Japan, he agreed to make *Dersu Uzala* in the Soviet Union, a movie he had long dreamed of making. The creative genius reflected in *Dersu Uzala* – which won the 1975 Academy Award for Best Foreign Language Film – was the outcome of Kurosawa's dramatic personal change. Like Dersu, Kurosawa had become a social outcast, wandering in the wilderness of his mind without human connection. And like Dersu, his "catastrophic change" (Bion, 1965) led to a second entry into human life, with all of its complexities, ironies, and limitations.

References

Bion, W. R. (1965). Transformations. In *Seven servants*. Aronson.

Schneider, J. A. (2005a). Dreaming the truth of experience: Heaven. *Psychoanalytic Review, 92*, 777–785.

Schneider, J. A. (2005b). Experiences in K and – K. *International Journal of Psychoanalysis, 86*, 825–839.

Schneider, J. A. (2007). Panic as a form of foreclosed experience. *Psychoanalytic Quarterly, 76*, 1293–1316.

10

Dreaming the Truth of Experience

Heaven

Dreams are, perhaps, the most truthful way we talk to ourselves. Daily, we face disturbing events that contradict what we believe to be true. Through their emotional impact, these experiences continue as thoughts and dreams during sleep and in waking unconscious dreaming (Bion, 1962). In this review, I consider the use of film as a way of dreaming the truth.

For Bion (1962, 1992), dreaming must involve unconscious psychological work by which we process elements of experience. We do not evaluate dreams as communications to ourselves or others based on the plausibility of their manifest content or rational logic. We rely, instead, on one of Freud's (1900/1953) criteria for dream interpretation – representability – which is the effectiveness of the dream images to convey emotional experience. Dreams do not need to represent in terms of accuracy, but, rather, they need the power to represent images that are true to unconscious life (not necessarily true to everyday life).

The film *Heaven* (2002) brings together the dream world and the world of film. Written by Krzysztof Kieslowski and directed by Tom Tykwer, *Heaven* begins by dropping us, the viewers, into an eerie, unsettling world of images and sounds. The experience is one of being untethered and ungrounded, floating above a terrain that seems neither real nor completely imaginary. We struggle in the opening scene to make sense of what is happening, and yet the colors, shapes, and sounds somehow stand on their own beyond an organizing narrative. We see a green film screen akimbo to the terrain below. We hear background noises – a continuous and monotonous whirring sound with muted human voices speaking in deliberate yet cautious tones – punctuated by suspenseful music.

In our effort to understand, we wonder (always uncertain) if this is a nightmare, a video arcade game, or perhaps a veteran's flashback to the Vietnam War seen through night-vision goggles. Suddenly the scene changes so that we realize we are looking at a flight simulator used to train pilots to fly helicopters. We are surprised to learn the scene was indeed a virtual reality, a mechanically enhanced dream of flying.

At this point in the movie, we are not allowed to look directly into the cockpit of the helicopter, but are given a view reflected off the lenses of the goggles of the pilot onto the helicopter windshield glass. (We are at least three times removed from what is happening and will remain so throughout the film.) The Italian pilot, Filippo

DOI:10.4324/9781003384601-10

(Giovanni Ribisi), is being trained to be a carabiniere (policeman) in the city of Turin. Filippo is told by the instructor to be careful about his helicopter's height, saying he can't just keep flying higher. Filippo then asks how high he can fly.

The second introductory scene is inside an apartment in Turin where someone is assembling a bomb. There is a nightmarish quality to this scene. The camera is at such close range, we cannot tell immediately whether it is a man or a woman, but we assume it is a terrorist. Next, the English-looking woman, Philippa Paccard (Cate Blanchett), takes the bomb to a high-rise office building where she gets past the secretary and into the office of an executive, Mr. Vendicci. Philippa places the bomb in Mr. Vendicci's wastebasket and slips away, stopping outside the building to make two telephone calls. The first is a life-saving ruse to get the secretary out of the office by falsely alerting her that her car alarm is wailing, and asking her if she can come down. The second call is to the Turin police to tell them that because they had ignored her previous calls and letters regarding Mr. Vendicci's destructive corruptness, she has taken matters into her own hands and placed a bomb in his office. After confessing her crime, she gives the police her name, making every effort to pronounce it clearly. We realize then that Philippa is not a terrorist.

While we watch Philippa making her calls, we are also shown, simultaneously, a father and his two young daughters heading toward the office elevator. Then, to our horror, we see the cleaning lady with the wastebasket from Vendicci's office on her cart join the father and daughters in the elevator. As we see Philippa taking an escalator down to the subway, we also see the office elevator going up. Then, for a moment, we are shown a still shot of the elevator doors followed by an explosion that rips the doors open. We are stricken and hope for a shift in perspective that renders all of this a horrible dream from which Philippa and we viewers will wake up.

It is as if the movie begins twice with two dreams, once in the fantasy world of the flight simulator and next in the nightmarish world of Philippa's apartment, with no obvious connection between the two. These two scenes introduce us to the two main characters of the film – whose names are nearly identical (Filippo and Philippa) – and to the film's main theme by way of our experience as viewers: the triumph of truth over reason and fact, and the centrality of truth to human experience. These opening scenes set us up to be surprised by the fact that we are sympathetic to characters initially at odds with what we are accustomed to believing to be a fundamental human truth. It is wrong to take the lives of innocents in terrorist attacks. The movie raises questions of truth, both directly in the plot and script, and indirectly in the screenplay, background music, and visual effects.

Like the opening session in an analysis, or the epigraph to a paper, the opening scene of *Heaven* is a condensed version of all that follows; and what follows always refers back to the opening scene. This film technique is used masterfully in *Heaven*, where the opening credits are given only after the tone is set through the drama of the opening scenes.

In the helicopter scene, we join Filippo's confusion in identifying what is true as he follows his instructions from the flight instructor. Our confusion is well-founded because this is a flight simulator, and like Filippo, who is being compliant with the instructor, we are being compliant at this point with our "internal master," that is, our associations to similar events and experiences. The reflected view we are allowed through his lenses is like a projective identification, a distorted representation that bears an unknown relationship to the truth. We are forced to wait "to see" what sort of truth we are involved in.

We are further unsettled in the scenes that follow to discover that we unwittingly have already identified with and are sympathetic to Philippa in spite of our having witnessed her murderous acts. We unwittingly become part of the scene in a way, and only in hindsight do we realize that we have given up our "selves" and our "truths" as we have known them. Later, after Philippa's plan to murder Vendicci backfires and she has a chance to escape, she is unwavering in her resolve to try again until she is successful in murdering him. Surprisingly, as viewers, we do not change the way we experience Philippa at this point; instead we find we are sympathetic to her killing this man. We are having the very strange experience of feeling that human life is no longer as sacred to us, and we are so powerfully drawn to vengeance.

We learn that Philippa is a British teacher living in Turin, where she teaches English to children. Her husband and at least one of her students died as a result of illegal drugs dealt by a business executive and drug kingpin, Mr. Vendicci. Philippa's repeated efforts to get help are ignored by the Turin police because of their complicity with Mr. Vendicci.

Believing that the bomb blast has killed Vendicci, Phillipa makes no effort to evade the police and, in a matter-of-fact way, confesses her crime to them and is arrested. During her hearing, we learn that Filippo is the court stenographer as well as the son of the former chief of police and a carabiniere-in-training. When Philippa refuses to testify in Italian, Filippo (again, surprisingly) inserts himself in the conversation asking if he can interpret, and they carry on the interrogation. There is a surreal – dream-like – quality about the convergence of coincidences in this scene. When she is told she is accused of causing an explosion in an office building, which has cost the lives of four persons, Philippa looks fully startled. Covering her mouth with astonishment, trembling and weeping, she utters the word "four" and then "quarto," speaking English and Italian lest there be a mistake, but also facing the horrible truth. She looks dumbfounded to learn she has killed four innocent people, including two children, and she pleads that she had wanted to kill Mr. Vendicci, the man who controlled the drug scene. It was because of him that schoolchildren and her husband had died. The head of the interrogation team replies that it was because of her that four people died. Now we, as viewers, are fully caught up in Philippa's nightmare. We cannot fully take in the enormity of the killing for which she is responsible.

Philippa falls to the floor, fainting from the shock. As a doctor pulls up Philippa's sleeve for a shot, Filippo holds her hand and looks into her eyes and seems to fall in love with her. She opens her eyes and asks where she is. He replies that she is with carabinieri. And she responds asking who he is. He says he is carabiniere. She is full of self-recrimination and replies that she is sorry. Is Philippa able to take in what she has done? We are unsure.

In the courtroom, Filippo looks awestruck as he is transformed – without questioning or doubting his experience – by Philippa, who is the truth, the O for what is happening. (O is the absolute – inarticulate and unknowable – universal human truth "and is who we are in dreaming" Bion, 1970; Ogden, 2004a, p. 292.) In so doing, he too "becomes the truth." Filippo devises an escape plan for the two of them, which at first seems to be of little interest to Philippa. His plan includes taking temporary sanctuary overnight in the attic of the court building. As time goes on, escape takes on meaning for Philippa as a necessary step in her renewed focus on killing Mr. Vendicci: that murder is the only important thing in life for her. Filippo then assists Philippa by getting Mr. Vendicci to come to the police station and supplies her with a pistol. Once face to face with Mr. Vendicci, she shoots him in the head. (Again, we wonder if this is real or if it is a dream of Philippa's.) The following morning, they escape from police headquarters in the back of a milk delivery truck and make their way to Tuscany.

Filippo's progressively intense identification with Philippa is evident when they appear in their identical disguises: a white T-shirt with blue jeans. They both speak in English. When they have their hair shorn to the scalp, the two have virtually become one. Their "disguise" is of a complex sort: It does not cover or hide the truth; it transcends everyday reality as do dreams, and reveals a truth that transcends what is generally held to be true. (Their "disguises" cause them to stand out – almost as aliens – for the viewer, but not for the other characters in the film such as the carabinieri, because they are no longer real; they are, at most, figures in a dream.) For Filippo and Philippa, details such as gender do not matter. Names do not matter. (On the train to Tuscany, Philippa tells Filippo that she doesn't even know his name.) Everything about Filippo and Philippa is true. There is no skirting or bending the truth. It is not enough to say they are honest; they are honesty, a simple un-self-conscious honesty. Everything they say to one another is true to their experience of themselves, of one another, of the world, and yet, they are not real, ordinary, flesh-and-blood people.

Philippa and Filippo enter the town square in Montepulciano where there are two churches. In one, a wedding is taking place, and in the other, Philippa confesses her sins to Filippo. She confesses that she has lied to her mother and sister and was once unfaithful to her husband. Only after confessing these sins against truth does she confess that four people died because of her (she leaves out the fifth, Mr. Vendicci). But she goes on to say that she shot a defenseless person, but what Filippo did not know was that she had ceased to believe. He asks her what she has ceased to believe. She responds that she has ceased to believe in sense, in justice, and in life. Philippa seems to leave her dream world momentarily, becoming more of a person at this point in the film.

The background music and quick segues from scene to scene – from city to country to rooftops to courtyards – set a gripping pace. The music provides a suspenseful and haunting background. Sharply registered piano notes are interjected into the slow, soulful, yet sorrowful pulse of the violin melody. The music appeals directly to our unconscious sensibilities and bolsters our response to the way truth is becoming disentangled from fact. The different camera angles and changing speeds and the eerie music each offer different "vertices" (Bion, 1965) to our experience. Truth and fact are becoming separate vertices as they are in dreams, which remain truthful no matter how the truth is disguised.

The filming is exquisite and beautiful. The "space camera system" is used from a helicopter, which has the capacity to give the camera-work a slow, strong, and steady movement in spite of the jagged vibrations of the helicopter. This system keeps the camera perpetually in balance, resulting in visual fluidity that has a dream-like, ethereal quality.

Each time we become immersed in the details of the story, the camera's "eye" moves high above the cityscape of Turin, a place from which we see a maze of red-tiled roofs and courtyards, but no details, no people. As a result of this technique, which removes us from the details and allows us to see things from a distant vantage point, we lose the rough edges. This stands in contrast to the opening scene where the camera is noticeably askew, and nothing seems natural, almost as if it is a fantasy. Then, Filippo and the viewer are trying to grasp the facts. Now, Filippo and the viewer do not care about "the facts"; the world is as it is as in a dream; nothing needs to be figured out, mastered, or understood.

The truth of a traditional wedding scene in the Montepulciano plaza church is juxtaposed with the truth being lived by Filippo and Philippa. It is not that the wedding is false. Nor is the family dinner scene Filippo and Philippa (and the viewer) later watch through a window. But Filippo and Philippa are living a different form of truth, one that is being created by the film. The convincing creation of this truth is the achievement of the film.

Truth as embodied by Philippa is at once strange and otherworldly yet completely natural. Despite so much that runs counter to the viewer's preconception of what is good and truthful, Filippo sensed there was another truth to the situation – a truth beyond revenge, murder, and morality. This is portrayed in a conversation when Philippa asks Filippo why he helped her escape. He replies that his brother (who is one of Philippa's students) likes her the most, and has said she is a good person. Filippo responds that he believed his brother. There was something that remained true about her despite the fact that she had murdered five people. What she did was morally indefensible, but why do Filippo and the viewer not condemn her for it? Surprisingly, we have become complicit in her killing of innocent children. Perhaps we justify our complicity because we feel we are in a dream, and we know dreams cannot be evil.

As court stenographer, Filippo's duty was to be as exact, objective, impartial, and as emotionally removed as possible – an illusory idea. When he volunteered to interpret for Philippa, he took the first step in transforming himself to become not a translator but an interpreter. He became more subjective, deciding how to express the nuances of Philippa's and the judge's statements. It is in this scene that he opens himself to Philippa's version of integrity and truth. By his interpretations, he speaks to "what is true to her emotional experience" (Ogden, 2003, p. 596) – not just to facts, but bringing an understanding to the situation beyond "just the facts." As interpreter, he processes all versions of what is true (see "binocular vision," Bion, 1970, and "truth instinct," Grotstein, 2004; Schneider, 2003, 2004), allowing him to become the O of the experience – the dreammaker. Philippa led Filippo to evolve a mind – a dream life – through his receptivity of her "evolution of O" (Bion, 1970). Bion conceptualizes dreaming as unconscious psychological work, and Ogden (2004b) has further defined the concepts of nightmares as interrupted dreams and night terrors as the inability to dream.

Filippo's integrity and truth are tested when, as interpreter in the courtroom, he must translate Philippa's words admitting she found a bag with a key and a note in the bathroom, which described a part of their escape plan. Despite his horror that she is giving away the escape plan, Filippo interprets verbatim what she says (the viewer shares the concern expressed in Filippo's face). When the magistrate asks what she said, he says absolutely honestly, that in the bathroom she had found a bag, a note, and a key. Shortly afterward Filippo is relieved to realize that, in fact, Philippa is talking about something else (an event that occurred weeks earlier with similar components but unrelated to their escape plot) and that their plan is intact. It seems that Philippa is living in dream-time.

Filippo's transformation demonstrates how he moves beyond (above) the reality of a policeman, a reality of law and justice passed down through generations. He performs the role of Hermes, the only god who could speak the language of both the gods and mortals. It was Hermes who accompanied Orpheus, who "dared more than any other man ever dared for his love." He took the fearsome journey to the underworld to bring back his deceased wife Eurydice, and in his journey he was accompanied by Hermes, "the solemn guide of the dead, the divine herald who led the souls down to their last home" (Hamilton, 1942, p. 35). Hermes, in a reversal of task, was leading the mortal from the land of the dead to the land of the living, a task that could be accomplished in a dream but not in reality or even in myth. Similarly, Filippo's task in *Heaven* was to transport himself and Philippa from the realm of the mortal to the world of the gods. He dreams of doing so in the poignant final scene, where he and Philippa commandeer a police helicopter, and he flies it straight up into the sky until it disappears. Filippo breaks the laws of natural science and again enters the realm of dreams.

There is something almost god-like in Filippo's response to Philippa's conviction. He was not distracted from her embodiment of truth by "details" such as the deaths of five people, as if they were only the manifest content of her attempts to dream the death of her husband. Rather, he seems to evolve over the course of the film into an omniscient god viewing all that is true for all living and nonliving things from the beginning to the end of time – the truth of the impossibility of fully dreaming terrible loss.

References

Bion, W. R. (1962). *Learning from experience*. Basic Books.

Bion, W. R. (1965). *Transformations*. Jason Aronson.

Bion, W. R. (1970). *Attention and interpretation*. Tavistock.

Bion, W. R. (1992). *Cogitations*. Tavistock.

Freud, S. (1953). The interpretation of dreams. In J. Strachey (Ed. & Trans.), *The standard edition of the complete psychological works of Sigmund Freud* (24 Vols., Vol. 5, pp. 339–405). Hogarth Press (Original work published 1900).

Grotstein, J. S. (2004). "The light militia of the lower sky": The deeper nature of dreaming and phantasying. *Psychoanalytic Dialogues*, *14*(1), 99–118.

Hamilton, E. (1942). *Mythology*. Little Brown.

Ogden, T. H. (2003). What's true and whose idea was it? *International Journal of Psychoanalysis*, *84*, 593–606.

Ogden, T. H. (2004a). An introduction to the reading of Bion. *International Journal of Psychoanalysis*, *85*, 285–300.

Ogden, T. H. (2004b). This art of psychoanalysis: Dreaming undreamt dreams and interrupted cries. *International Journal of Psychoanalysis*, *85*, 857–877.

Schneider, J. A. (2003). Janus-faced resilience in the analysis of a severely traumatized patient. *Psychoanalytic Review*, *90*, 865–867.

Schneider, J. A. (2004). Experiences in K and –K. *International Journal of Psychoanalysis*, *86*, 825–839.

Index

acting in the body 49
Ali Baba: Arabian Knights 85
aliveness 72, 75, 102
alpha elements: to deal with thoughts 30; processing emotional experience 16, 18–19; theory of thinking 40; transformed into meaningful experience 37; and trauma 94, 104
alpha function: linked to thinking 37, 38
analytic dyad 31, 34, 36, 42; and recognizing basic assumptions 44
Aristotle: dream is way mind works in sleep 18, 46
asymbolic experience: and psychosomatic disorders 60–61, 67
autistic contiguous: assigning meaning to experience 108; evacuation of internal experience 116; mode of generating experience sensation dominated way 59; and understanding eating disorders 107–111
autistic object(s): autosensuous 108–113; safety generating sensory impression 61; shapes to be controlled 114

basic assumptions: in the analytic dyad 42–44; dependency group 36; elements 36–40; fight-flight 36; pairing group 36
being dreamt 1; co-created dream thoughts 4
beta elements: get evacuated 37; mentalization 58; stimuli 61–62; talking about unthought matters 30; trauma denuded of meaning 94; unassimilated 40; unavailable for dreaming 104; unlinked formation of dreams 16–19, 25
Bick, Esther: second-skin formation 57–58, 61n4, 109

binocular vision: analyst awareness for basic assumptions in dyads 44; instrument of observation (thinking) 32
Bion, Francesca: Introduction—Bion's autobiographical essays 32; "loaded with honors and sunk" 41
Bion, Wilfred R. 1–5, 9–11; basic assumption groups 36; dream-thoughts as two versions 12–13; dream as works in progress 19, 21; emotional experience 16–18; group mentality 29; intelligible field of study 31; personal experience with groups 41; protomental matrix concept 39; re-conception of dreaming 15–19; work groups 38–39
Britton, Ronald 39; Bion's quote about home for wild idea 42
Bruch, Hilde: disorders of separation individuation 106–107

communication: bodily 6; extra-sensory 2–3, 19; nonverbal 55, 57, 73; open 43, 48, 52; realistic 35, 40; symbolic 64, 74
conscious and unconscious mind 2; waking-dreaming 3
contact barrier 3; moving freely from conscious to unconscious 19
continuity of being 79; disturbance in 107–108

De M'Uzan, Michel: acting in the body 49
dental stimulus dream: Freud's metaphor for repression 14–15
Dersu Uzala (Kurosawa) 118; unlikely friendship and loss of friendship 122–123
dream experience: in a group 5–6

dreaming 1–26; and ANS activity 59; Bion's to be alive 94–95; as a containing function 18; imageless dreams 105; nightmares and night terrors 129; patient into existence 1; talking as 1; truthful self-talk 124–127
dreams: as mental indigestion 20; as works in progress 1, 9, 19, 21, 26; as works in stasis 21
dream-thoughts: dream content 12–13, 16–18, 22
dream-work: Freud's 9–15

eating disorder: clinical illustration 111–112, 115; Ogden, Tustin theoretical formulations 106–109
ego: concept of 10, 30; splitting 110; weakness 106; see also superego
emotional experience: disturbing 21, 24–26, 48, 79, 95; perceptions of 18–20; processing of 4, 9–11; working with 15–17
evacuation 3; basic assumptions encoded 40, 94; and beta elements 16
evolution of O: dream-life and receptivity 129

Fairbairn, William Ronald Dodds: internal object relations theory 109–111; transforming bad object into good 106
Freud, Sigmund: actual neurosis and panic 62; analyst work interpreting dream 25; dream interpretation by analyst 1–3; dreamwork reconsidered 9–15; explanations of eating disorders 106; importance of not perceiving reality 80; influence on Bion's groups 31–34; mind working in sleep 18–19; self begins in body 116; trauma and economic metaphor 94–95

Green, Andre: negative hallucination 88
gregariousness: enhances survival and evolution 35; ever-present influence of personality 36; strongest urge in humans (Trotter) 33
Grotstein, James: overview of splitting 76n1; review theory of dreaming 104n3
groupishness: Bion's concept of 29–31, 34
group mentality 5, 29, 30, 34, 38–39, 42; significant in all individual analyses 44
group psychology 8, 34, 44, 58
guardians of sleep 11

hallucination 7; and disturbing psychic reality 23; as evacuation of beta elements 62; experience hallucinated in sleep 17; as extreme form of –K 90–91
hallucinatory: dreaming 4; elements 17, 23; experience 21, 25; hallucinatory parts of dreams 21–22; images as vision hallucinations 23; parts 5
healthy splitting 6, 39; healthy use of K 6; mental activity as protection 64–66, 69
herd instinct: Trotter, humans as political animals 31–34, 36
herd mentality 40, 43

individual psychology and group influence 42–44
infant: autistic objects perceived as sensory impressions 108–110; childhood psychic trauma 95; infant separateness 80; reputation as environmental mother 115
instinct: gregariousness a fourth instinct 30–33; group instinct latent in individuals 44; herd and Trotter 32–33; inborn need to be a group member 29–30; maternal failure to hold 48; need to get to know (K) 79; separate vertices in dreams 128
internalize the bad object to control in eating disorders (Fairbairn) 110

Janus-faced resilience: pathological underbelly of resilience 93

Klein, Melanie: concept of projective identification 3; eating disorders 107–110; failure of symbol formation 35–36
knowing/not knowing (K/-K): aim to make unthinkable thinkable 79–81; analysts negative capability 91; defensive need not to know 89; healthy use of –K not driven by envy 6–7; -K as self-protective 90–91
Kurosawa 7, 118; Japanese filmmaker 122–123

learn from experience: the capacity to think 37
lived by one's experience: difference from living one's dreaming 7, 108
living one's dreaming 2, 7

maternal reverie: in childhood trauma 95
McDougall, Joyce: disaffected states
    52, 107
Meltzer, Donald: adhesive identification 109,
    113
mental microscope: use in psychoanalysis 32
mind body: Bion's least acknowledged
    contribution 29
multiple vertices: Bion's thinking on
    co-operation 37–38; holding multiple
    points of view simultaneously 32

non-psychotic: always making meaning of
    experience 18; part of every dream 26;
    personality 7; use of –K 79; when not able
    to think 91n4

Oedipus: what did Oedipus know and not
    know   80–81
Ogden, Thomas: autistic-contiguous mode
    of generating experience 59; concept of
    analytic third 67; emphasis on process of
    dreaming 9; non-experience 52; patient
    knew but did not know   91; primitive
    internal object relationships 106–110;
    re-conceptualized dreaming 1–3; tension
    between influence and originality 45;
    undreamable experience 17–18
operational thinking: extension of action 59;
    going beyond in a dream 60; remove from
    the internal psychic world 49

panic disorder: asymbolic experiences 60–61;
    as a form of foreclosure 48–49, 56–58
paradigm shift 3; dreaming 9–10; thinking
    about groups 31
paranoid-schizoid: dimension and
    sensation-based experience 114; splitting
    as a facet of 6
pathological splitting: distinguished from
    healthy splitting 6; a generative space
    64–73; stalemated polarization and
    countertransference 75
primary psychoanalytic function of mind:
    Bion and dreaming 15; pursuit of
    truth 25
projective identification: defense used in
    paranoid-schizoid position 116n3; denial
    of rage 66–67; eating disorders 108;
    emotional experience not transformed by
    alpha 62; healthy objective identification
    79, 115; Klein and omnipotent phantasy

3; psychic evacuation and communication
    16, 18, 20
protomental: bodily sensory 30; may become
    physical or illness 40–41; pre-empt
    thinking 39; turning into mental 43,
    58, 36
psychosomatic disorder 59–60
psychotic 4; Klein, individual's psychotic
    anxieties 35; magical thinking and
    psychotic reveries 23–24; negative
    hallucination communication 91;
    nonpsychotic part of personality 26;
    undreamed parts 16–18

Rank, Otto: and Freud's theory of
    dreaming 14–15
resilience: childhood drawback 7;
    double-edged quality underbelly 93,
    110
reverie 22, 24, 50, 53, 59, 70; use of
    countertransference analysis 74–75;
    waking dreams of analyst 2–6
royal road to a knowledge of the
    unconscious 13

sensation-based shapes: in immediate
    environment 58
sense impressions: alpha function 16, 30, 58
superego 30, 34
symbolic thinking: in panic disorders 55; in
    work groups 40

thinking: primary-process 3; secondary
    process 21; the shape of a dream 21
Trotter, Wilfred: group mentality 32;
    influence on Bion 31–37, 42,
    44–45
truth instinct: human beings "to get to
    know" 79, 128
Tustin, Frances: sensation-dominated
    skin-surface experiences 106–109

unconscious: dreaming 1–8; Freud's
    dream-work 10–13; lived experience for
    unconscious dreaming 25–26, 36, 38, 40,
    58, 66; splitting 73–75
undigested facts: emotional experience
    remains unlinked 16, 61
undreamable 1; dream the undreamable
    24–25; examples of 4–5, 17–18, 79, 48
undreamt: dream 17, 20; unsayable
    unthinkable parts 21–22, 26

valency: tendency for humans to group
    together 36–38
verbal interpretations 4, 48; when premature
    in some analyses 58–59

waking dreaming 2, 5, 7, 25; need to develop
    thinking 37–40, 95
Wallace, Elizabeth M.: individual psychology
    and basic assumption groups in training 43

Winnicott, D. W. environmental mother
    115; matrix of transference 115; play
    space 70
work group: in the analytic dyad
    42, 44; cooperative endeavor
    pursuing common purpose
    38–40
working without words: unspeakable
    experience in the body 49

Printed in Dunstable, United Kingdom